"Happy Father's Day"
Daddy

from Karen & Carla

HOUSE PLANTS

For the indoor gardener

By the Editors of
Better Homes & Gardens

Orange clivia—related to the amaryllis blooms indoors in winter, spends its summers outdoors.

Contents

Spring bulbs bloom early—indoors. Tulips and daffodils gleam against the green of foliage plants.

Introduction

To all who delight in the daily presence of green and growing things, this book is dedicated. In it are advice and information for both novice and experienced gardener. Pictures and text show how to select the right plants from your florist or at your greenhouse, how to display them decoratively, how to keep them growing luxuriantly.

Especially is this book directed to you who lament the lack of a "green thumb," or who have been led to believe there's a deal of mystery surrounding success with house plants. Here, simply stated, is basic information to dispel the myths, to inform you concerning the whys and wherefores of healthy house plants—how to light, water, feed, pot, and multiply them.

Here, too, are handsome pictures of hundreds of varieties of plants you can choose from. Some will be old friends; others will be strangers—exciting additions to your collection of favorites. Many of the photographs contain new ideas on ways of using plants to bring a fresh and exciting look to the familiar rooms of your home—grouped for mass effect, placed for bold accent.

One of the joys of indoor gardening is that it's never out of season. House plants, with glossy, green foliage or bright colored blooms, can keep memories of spring and summer alive, no matter what the calendar may say or how the cold winds blow.

Use this book through all the months of the year for ideas, for inspiration, for guidance in growing house plants that will increase the beauty of your home, add pleasure to your daily life.

The Editors

Better Homes and Gardens

Chapter 1

The decorative use of house plants

Plants are ornaments for the rooms you live in. Of course you enjoy them just for themselves. But you increase your pleasure by selecting and placing plants where they will be tasteful room accents—the finishing touch that completes an effective decorating plan.

Perhaps you seek boldness of form or leaf pattern. Or maybe color is the major consideration. Whatever you want done decoratively, there are plants that will do it for you, and grow happily under the conditions of light and warmth you can provide. The choices are many.

Depending on the size and style of the particular room, its colors, the space available, you'll consider whether you want to mass a number of plants in one impressive group, or spotlight a single star in the strategic location that makes it a focus of interest.

Think, too, in terms of scale. A big expanse of plain wall demands a plant or group of plants of generous dimensions. But if you have a small area to decorate, choose a gem that asks to be looked at close up, that will be in good proportion to its setting.

In the pages to follow, explore the treasury of ideas on plants and ways to use them decoratively in your home. Decide on the effect you want; then choose the plants that will create it for you easily.

Large-leaved plants, orange blooms add zest →

The well-known decorator in whose home this picture was taken uses showy foliage silhouettes to enliven a wall of drapery, flowering plants to reinforce the desert-orange color accents.

Group your plants for bigger eye appeal

The mass effect of a handsome group of plants satisfies a universal love of the spectacular. Any one plant in the group may be attractive in its own right, though possible to overlook if alone. But put several together—in the right setting—and you just can't ignore their presence.

There's more than one way to group plants, of course. A well-chosen pair is often just what you want. An assortment of many varieties gives the same pleasurable thrill as looking into a florist's shop. On the following pages you'll see these and more ideas for achieving the mass effect.

Choose plants according to their setting

To show off a group of plants effectively, you need enough space to keep it from appearing crowded. And if the plants contain a sharp color contrast—like the red-green scheme pictured—you also need a neutral setting. Against a vivid background, substitute plants with lots of white in foliage and flowers. Or try the wide range of greens only which foliage plants offer.

Look for contrasts of color, texture, form

Some plants have shiny foliage. Others have a furry or velvety finish to their leaves. There are big, pointed shapes as well as rounded, pierced, or lacelike leaves to choose from. And greens go from palest chartreuse to almost black tones.

Get variety in size, too. Choose some tall, some short plants to combine. Place the taller ones toward the back, shorter ones in front, so that all can be seen to best advantage.

For a starter, try a few of these plant combinations: yellow, bunch-flowered chrysanthemums made to look even more flowery when backed by a good dieffenbachia; African-violets that will appear still daintier with a rugged jadeplant for background; ferns that look like green lace when contrasted with the solid foliage of big-leaved philodendrons or rubber plants.

←
Amaryllis and caladium supply a burst of color

The trumpet shape of amaryllis blooms complements heart shape of fancy-leaved caladium plants. Both come in a range of reds and whites that makes them good companions; both are bulb plants to grow indoors in late winter — just when you respond most to color.

Tea cart substitutes for window ledge

Pink azaleas, pink and white hyacinths, red and white tulips, yellow daffodils, plus some African-violets make a gorgeous color load for a tea cart that's easy to wheel to other room locations. In full bloom, these plants last longer out of sun.

A window garden is

Flowering plants in a kaleidoscope of hues can be the exclamation point in rooms that are furnished largely with neutral tones. And nothing's a more effective color cure in the winter months than a window garden full of bright, blooming plants.

Some—like poinsettias, azaleas, and cyclamen plants—must be bought from the florist unless you have a home greenhouse. They'll keep considerably longer than most cut flowers, but can't last forever.

Others—such as African-violets and the everblooming begonias—will thrive through all twelve months of the year under average home conditions. Also, you can force your own crop of spring-flowering bulbs for a succession of colorful bloom indoors.

Combine flowering, foliage plants

An easy way to extend the impressiveness of a few flowering plants is to combine them with your faithful foliage performers. Two or three pots of bloom will bulk twice as large in a nest of handsome green.

The grouping across the page is a good example of how you can stretch the effect with foliage. Pink cyclamen, yellow and white azaleas, and red poinsettia are the only plants bought as seasonal accents. In combination with pink and purple African-violets, several varieties of foliage begonias and other year-round foliage plants, they look like twice as many.

Later chapters will tell you more about the right growing conditions for all the plants pictured here. Check individual requirements for light, water, and warmth to be sure the plants you want to combine will stay healthy and good-looking in home location you've chosen for a window garden.

Spring peeps out at a window sill

It's easy to force tulips and daffodils for an early indoor spring. Plant bulbs in clay pots; sink them outdoors in the fall. Then at the first thaw, bring indoors where they will bloom weeks earlier than their outdoor cousins.

the answer for rooms in need of color

Add flowering plants to foliage Azaleas, poinsettia and cyclamen move in with the foliage plants to brighten a winter window garden.

Vibrant color notes with blooming plants

If you like the dramatic emphasis that a living plant in bloom gives to a decorating scheme, plan ahead for it! Of course, you can buy beautiful seasonal flowering plants from your florist, and some can't be grown successfully except under greenhouse conditions. But there are many varieties which you can grow yourself.

In fall, you can lift and pot the late-blooming garden plants—chrysanthemums, for example—and bring them into the house to be enjoyed after frost. When faded, replace in garden if soil's not frozen. Otherwise, tie plastic bag around pot, store in cool, dark spot until spring.

Also in fall, you can plant spring bulbs in pots, sink them outdoors, and bring them inside for brilliant color accents long before the garden varieties have pushed their way through the winter-bound earth.

How to make blooms last

When you buy flowering plants from your florist, look for those which are full of buds. That way you'll have the pleasure of watching them swell and open, and it will be longer before they begin to fade.

It takes lots of moisture for a plant to produce blooms, so be sure to water faithfully while it is in bud and coming toward flowering. If you let the plant get completely dry at this time, flower buds may be damaged so seriously they'll never open.

In bitter winter weather, move the plants away from the window at night if there is danger of their frosting when house temperature drops. Or give them protection against the cold by pulling down the window shade; or slip a piece of heavy cardboard between the plants and the windowpane.

← *Sunny blooms to brighten winter*

Tulips, both double and single, and daffodils are easy to force for indoor bloom. Azaleas are miniature shrubs, handled by florists who offer reds (as here), pale pinks, whites. Choose color that does most to enhance your room scheme.

Mums complement a glossy begonia

Have sunshine in big splashes with yellow chrysanthemums. Pot up your garden variety or buy some from your florist, who also has bronzy-reds, lavenders, white. They bring you several weeks of easy-to-get color.

Showcases for indoor gardens

Take a tip from jewelers who know how to display their gems effectively, in brightly lighted windows. Plants, too, sparkle when they're set in the bright showcase of your windows. Light makes colors glow, and it's also good for the growth of the plants.

A window garden can be part of the architecture, as pictured across the page; or, it can be assembled on plant stands and in planters, as shown in the group of sketches you see below. Tailor your window garden to suit best window location in your home.

The most successful window garden will be the one that's planned to suit the plants it includes in regard to light, temperature, and water. If you have a suitable south window, you can grow almost any house plant. But east and west windows, too, get enough sun to please some of the most attractive members of the foliage plant family.

← Twin stands for a bay window

A pair of plant stands can put a garden in a bay window. Movable arms accommodate large, small pots of ivies, begonias, Boston and Holly ferns, African-violets. Use saucers under plants to avoid stains.

Tiered tables take little space →

Use a tiered table, a Lazy Susan, or a library step table to get this effect. Give a dish garden top position. Below, set small caladiums, striped peperomias, grape-ivies and African-violets or gloxinias in a variety of colors.

← A radiator top can be adapted

With a layer of insulation as protection (asbestos shingles will do), you can grow many warmth-loving plants on a radiator top. Keep an air space open above the radiator grille so air can circulate.

In central position is an aquarium (its glass sides trap moister air) planted with coleus, dieffenbachia, and African-violets. Sansevieria, jadeplant, necklace-vine in flanking plant boxes tolerate drier air.

An indoor-outdoor window garden

This window garden in two parts—inside and outside—is well worth planning for if you're about to build or remodel your home.

Evergreens fill the outdoor half, while the inner half blazes with flowering bulbs backed by luxuriant peppermint geraniums, a spotted dieffenbachia, and vining grape ivy.

Profile drawing at right shows deep gravel layer that supplies good drainage. Inside ledge is at right working height. Window faces south.

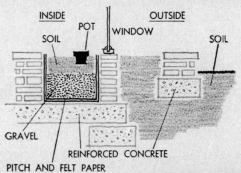

INSIDE   POT   OUTSIDE

SOIL   WINDOW   SOIL

GRAVEL

REINFORCED CONCRETE

PITCH AND FELT PAPER

Enjoy your potted plants without fear of watermarks

Set clay pots into waterproof jardinieres or adopt one of the protectors sketched below as a safeguard against stains from spilled water. Place large, difficult-to-move plants like palms and monstera pictured above on platforms equipped with casters. This way you can shift to other locations easily, without danger to you or to the plant.

GLASS PIEPLATE

ALUMINUM FOIL

VARNISHED CLAY SAUCER

LARGE TRAY WITH SEVERAL POTTED PLANTS

PLATFORM ON CASTERS

Beauty in a hurry with potted plants

You can give any room fresh glamor in a hurry with a group of potted plants. Their color, living beauty, dramatic looks have a decorative flair that's hard to equal.

For a big splash of color, group several potted plants in one spot. Do this with a few big ones like the mums across the page. Or use many small pots, inside a dish, tray, or other container, like the coleus you see below in a shining brass tub.

Be practical, too, about the way you display potted plants. Don't risk stained rugs or furniture by neglecting to supply good protection against spilled water. See how you can do this in several easy ways in the group of sketches below.

And don't expect potted plants to stay decorative forever. Some, like coleus, can be re-rooted from tip cuttings when they become spindly and unattractive.

Others, like potted mums, will fade and must be removed promptly when they do. If they are a winter-hardy variety, you can set them out in your garden. Otherwise, be ruthless about discarding them when they have passed their prime.

Coleus offers jewel tones

New sophistication for coleus (long a favorite because it's so easy to grow from cuttings) comes with a freshly dramatic setting.

Leave stocky plants in their pots, spread a layer of vermiculite or coarse sand in large, moistureproof container. Tilt outer pots so that foliage falls well over sides. Keep vermiculite or gravel wet, and the plants in good, strong light.

SET POTS IN SAND

TILT OUTER POTS

Color capsules for the winter-bound

*Amaryllis, philodendron
and azalea make a bright
group for winter enjoyment*

Amaryllis grow from large bulbs and are seemingly without a fixed time-table. If you like surprises, then amaryllis with huge trumpets of red, pink, or salmon are for you.

Cold-treated bulbs will bloom in-doors in time for Christmas. See the chapter on flowering plants for direc-tions on how to grow amaryllis and how to care for the bulbs after they bloom so they'll be ready to perform again the following year.

*It's a pure luxury but an
exciting experience to
have a real orchid plant*

Once they're budded, cattleya orchid plants are fairly rugged. Blooms last for weeks if kept in good light, out of sun.

Only if you supply greenhouse conditions of warmth and humi-dity will they bloom again.

Colorful companions are small forms of the Rex begonia.

← *Built-in window garden
features a burst of bloom
to contradict winter*

No pining for summer here! Not when you can put the color of real flowers into winter days.

This floor-level garden has a concrete slab base. It could be adapted to an older house with waterproof floor joints, nailing galvanized iron sheets securely between them to hold the sand.

To be admired at close range

For plants small and fascinating because of striking foliage patterns, or delicacy of blooms, setting is important. Give them top billing by placing them on an end table to be enjoyed at close range.

There's a host of fine plants that warrant a close look. Pictured are foliage begonias, African-violets, and white cyclamen. Among others you'll appreciate in a similar setting are gloxinias, bushy specimens of the everblooming begonia, and the not-too-tall spring flowering bulbs such as hyacinths or crocus in yellows, purples, white.

In the foliage family, try a Prayer Plant with pretty, chocolate-brown spots on its leaves, red- or white-nerved fittonia, the boldly veined aphelandra, coleus in bright hues, and several of the peperomias.

Slip pots into decorative containers that will protect table tops and harmonize with the style of room furnishings, whether Contemporary or Traditional.

Try a fresh combination of plants for special effect

There's an elegant simplicity about both these plants that makes them a good pair for step-table shelves.

Snowy-white blooms of cyclamen look even more ruffly next to the polished heart-shaped leaves of a Ruth Grant foliage begonia plant. Both the cyclamen in bloom and the begonia do best out of sunlight.

Stage a showy display with → tapestry-color begonias

Begonias are for north windows and other spots not in direct sun.

The two in the foreground are in the Rex group. The third plant, with rich, red-leather undersides and a satiny top is a Ruth Grant.

You can fit begonias into either a Traditional or Contemporary room by a change of their containers.

African-violets are worth a long gaze

Planted in a wire basket lined in moisture-holding sphagnum moss are nine African-violets, in assorted colors. Basket is set on a metal tray to protect table.

What lovelier way to display all those extra young plants that are so easy to grow from leaves.

A living plant with bold foliage

Anyone with an eye for interior decoration sees the job a large foliage plant can do if it's in the right setting. And as a living, growing decoration, it's doubly interesting.

See how well a big, healthy rubber plant serves to add an effective vertical line to a room where horizontals predominate. The contrast is natural and welcome.

In the room below, freshness is breathed into a warm decorating scheme by setting down a pair of cool, white caladium plants, their impressive, big leaves veined in green.

Take note of the wide variety of foliage plants shown on the following pages, which are big enough, striking enough to serve as focal points in well-decorated rooms.

Many of the plants you'll see will grow well in low-light situations. Others need more sun. Remembering that they are living things, choose the varieties that can stay healthy and good-looking, continue to grow under the room conditions you can offer.

The fancyleaf caladium grows from a tuber

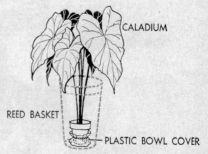

CALADIUM

REED BASKET

PLASTIC BOWL COVER

Available in many colors, some fancyleaf caladiums have pale pink or deeper rose marbling on their green leaves—to fit another room scheme.

Display your plants attractively, adapting the idea you see sketched just above.

Indiarubber tree adapts →
well to home conditions

Most common of rubber plants in the home, *Ficus elastica* withstands poor conditions of light, temperature, moisture. But it grows best in bright light or shade—not sun.

A husky plant like this one needs a sturdy base. Set it in a tub or jardiniere that suits the decorating scheme.

can perform as a room accent

One big, green plant looks lavish

Make a moss stick and grow your own vining plants on a totem

Moss stick will supply moist surface for growing a "totem pole" of Devil's ivy (scindapsus). See Chapter II for directions on how to make your own moss stick.

Monstera has majestic good looks

Aristocratic monstera is a native of South America which adapts surprisingly well to home growing conditions. Another climbing plant, it tolerates any exposure but direct sun. Grows best in a moist atmosphere.

← Dieffenbachia for upright foliage

Young plants of this Dieffenbachia Rudolph Roehrs make fine specimens to set down singly. Older plants go leggy but are still good for backgrounds; or they can be brought back to earth by the process of air-layering.

Totem shows off graceful foliage

Devil's ivy (mistakenly called variegated philodendron) is slower growing than standard philodendron which also does well on a moss stick. Stick kept moist helps supply the humidity which both need for healthy growth.

Hardy beauties

Any man with just a spark of interest in green and growing things will like to have a plant to decorate his office. It does wonders to dress up an austere interior without looking fussy.

Choose one with masculine manners and a rugged disposition—one that can withstand the adverse growing conditions that frequently prevail. There's apt to be low light and humidity, but there are plants that can tolerate these handicaps, continue to grow and stay attractive over a relatively long period of time.

Because growth is almost certain to be slow, it's best to select a mature plant that will look good from the start. Young ones may not increase their size rapidly enough to be satisfactory, unless used in a planter in combination with plants big enough to hold their own.

A foliage plant is your best choice for a man's office or den, both because it can

Easy-to-grow and colorful

Rhoeo discolor, "Moses-in-a-boat," has odd leaves that are green above, bright purple below. It tolerates low light for rather prolonged periods, but needs frequent watering.

For healthier plants, put a lamp near a planter to supplement daylight

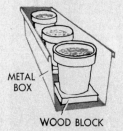

METAL BOX

WOOD BLOCK

One cause of failure with indoor planters is lack of sufficient bottom drainage. As a precaution, leave plants in their own pots and raise to desired height with wood blocks. Dieffenbachia, monstera and philodendron dubium in planter are all impressive in size and tolerate reduced light reasonably well. Fancy-leaf caladium provides seasonal splash of color.

for a man's office

get along with less light than most of the flowering varieties, and because it looks more like a man's choice. Also, it is interesting all year long, not just when seasonally in bloom.

Strong leaf outlines rather than fine or lacy ones will be best. The philodendron family, several varieties of begonia, dieffenbachias, fiddleleaf fig, rubber plants are all good in this respect.

For greatest appeal, keep scale in mind. Choose a plant that is small enough—or big enough—to suit its setting. For a desk top, you'll want one of lesser proportions than those which decorate a big area.

Set large specimens on the floor, in tubs, making sure they have enough space around them so they won't look crowded or interfere with through traffic, or be damaged by being brushed against.

Well-selected containers also enhance. Look for colors and shapes that complement both the plant and the total office decorating scheme. Style of a container, too, should harmonize in spirit with the room—Contemporary or Traditional.

Here's a rugged plant for a man's office or study

Fiddleleaf fig is tall-growing, has a handsome form. It needs frequent sunning if located away from direct light. Dust leaves with damp cloth.

← For philodendron fanciers, here's a new variety

One of the newer vines on the market is *Philodendron andreanum*. Give it bright light for healthy growth, and something that it can climb on.

If the new leaves are progressively smaller, plant needs more light.

More good performers that suit

It's fun to watch this little plant grow

Pick-a-back plant (*tolmeia menziesi*) gets its' common name from its way of producing new plants at the base of old leaves, so that they appear to be riding on the back of the mother plant. It's easy to have more of this one; peg old leaf to soil until new roots grow.

A smaller plant can give a big effect

Young plants of Rex begonias have gem-like tones of violet and blue-reds mixed with green that fit subtly into almost any decorating scheme. They're a good choice for an office since they don't like direct sun, and do well in reduced light situations over a long time.

masculine tastes

Once a man discovers the cheer, color, and freshness that pot plants can contribute to his private domain of office or den, he'll want them always on hand. For mere pennies a day, nothing does more to give a lift to the spirits, smartness to the decor.

Not every plant is suited to office life, if it's characterized by poor light, bad ventilation, or overheating. But there are a number that can withstand poor conditions for fairly long periods, and many which are inexpensive enough so they can be replaced by fresh ones when they lose their looks.

On these pages we show you examples of the bargains and the "toughies." All are foliage plants worth knowing better; all are graceful without being so dainty as to look out-of-place in a man's world.

Where to place plants in offices

Don't think every plant has to go into a window. In many offices this is impossible in any case—because of heating and ventilating installations located beneath them.

A lamp near a plant will do much to boost the light supply, and will give it a more dramatic setting at the same time.

Plants look well on desks, bookcases, storage cabinets, or on the floor—providing they are big enough to warrant this. A tub or totem planting should be about three feet tall for on-the-floor placement.

For vining plants, a wall bracket is appropriate. Many ivies, philodendrons, some peperomias, and several members of the *cissus* family, such as the Kangaroo vine, are outstanding against a wood-paneled or plain, painted wall typical in offices.

Whatever the office location you decide on for a plant, use as much care in selecting an appropriate container as you would in choosing an accessory for your home.

The wife who presents her husband with a plant for his office might do much to insure its prolonged life and good looks by sending along a note for the secretary with brief instructions about light, watering and dusting. Including a small extra plant for the secretary's own desk would be double insurance of good plant care!

English ivy thrives in bright, moist surroundings, but it's inexpensive to replace if you can't meet these needs.

Fatshedera lizei has big, five-lobed leaves resembling ivy, but it is an upright shrub, good for a floor planter.

Dieffenbachias make fine, decorative plants — both attractive and tolerant of less-than-perfect growing conditions.

Dividing space with greenery

Plants can be more than good to look at. They can be functional, too, when you grow them in a room divider where they are part of a substitute wall that separates space.

The modern house, built on an open plan, often includes planter-dividers as a basic design element. Older homes, too, use dividers to make two rooms of one.

Because they will be so prominently displayed, it's doubly important to have only the glossiest, healthiest of plants in your di-vider. Success is most certain if you'll choose plants that don't demand sunlight for survival. Chinese evergreen, Trileaf wonder, philodendrons, and sansevierias, are a few of the foliage plants which are obliging in a reduced light location.

Take pains, if your planter has no bottom drainage hole, to put in a good layer of pebbles or broken crockery before you set plants in place. Overwatering is a common source of trouble that this step overcomes.

Separate space aesthetically with plants and paintings in a dramatic setting

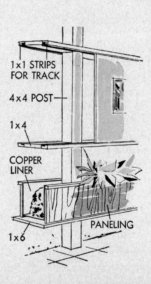

1 x 1 STRIPS FOR TRACK

4 x 4 POST

1 x 4

COPPER LINER

1 x 6

PANELING

Paintings and plants are natural companions for a divider designed to separate the dining and living areas of one large room.

Sketch at left shows construction details, including a copper lining for plant box, with side paneling to match other woodwork in the room.

Design would be improved if provision were made to install fluorescent tubes immediately above plants.

The extra amount of illumination thus supplied would do much to insure a long and healthy life for plants in a dimly lighted situation such as this.

Floor-level planter

If your front door opens directly into the living room, this floor planter can subtly indicate an entrance area, separate from the rest of the room.

A handyman could easily build one like it to the dimensions you need. Give it a metal liner.

Rubber plant, monstera, sansevieria, philodendron fill it attractively.

A series of open shelves in simple, bookcase style, carry a collection of ivies and African- violets. If all light comes from one side, turn plants regularly so their growth will be even.

The architectural use of plants

Contemporary architecture often sets such a chastely simple background for living that it demands the inclusion of contrasting decorative forms for a harmonious whole.

To make certain that plants will be used and placed for best effect, the architect frequently builds a planter into the house, indicating the place where plants should be put to complement clean, straight lines.

The sculptured look of big foliage plants is nowhere more striking and appropriate than in such a setting. Leaf patterns against the sweep of a plain wall become much more than a pleasant afterthought.

In such a setting, scale is a prime consideration. Notice that in the room pictured below, anything but tall, bold-leaved plants would look insignificant.

In those across the page, the need for height is reduced, but leaves must be big enough to be seen at a distance before plantings can have proper importance.

Plants reinforce a suggested separation of living-dining areas

Philodendron and dieffenbachia in a brick planter which is an extension of fireplace wall soften the lines and improve effect of a room divider. Plant box on mantel above lets philodendron vine downward gracefully to join the plants at the lower level.

Foliage gives fresh, inviting air to an entrance hall

Several varieties of philodendron, a palm, and two tall rubber plants make interesting patterns against the window, offer both an outdoor and an indoor welcome to this home.

The plants used here are suited to growing next to a window of any but a south exposure, since all like light but not direct sun over a long period of time. East or north are most desirable exposures for this type planter.

← Contemporary interior makes a functional use of plants

This modern version of the conservatory brings plants into the living room, uses them as ornamentation.

Concealed fixtures supply necessary light for plant health, make them look dramatic at the same time.

Philodendron dubium climbs on tree branches for background height; dieffenbachia takes a center-front spot, with dracaena planted at right and in a floor-level planter in hallway.

Cutleaf foliage pattern brings good contrast to a sleekly simple interior

An important totem pole planting of monstera in a container with oriental lines introduces pattern to a setting where the simplicity of a black and white color scheme plus straight lines is a dominant theme.

The exotic look of this plant has made it very popular as an accent to Contemporary architecture. Its size makes it suitable for use as the one, bold ornament to contrast with its unornamented background.

A native of tropical America, the monstera is a climbing plant, perfect to grow on a totem. Enormous leaves (some are over a foot long) are deeply slit and some are pierced with a number of holes along either side of the midrib.

Plants this big are in the luxury class, but you can start with young ones and have a large one in time.

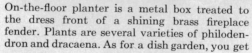

On-the-floor planter is a metal box treated to the dress front of a shining brass fireplace fender. Plants are several varieties of philodendron and dracaena. As for a dish garden, you get the most harmonious effect by including—and grouping—some tall, some short plants. Unless the plants receive daylight, provide for daily artificial lighting to keep them alive.

make welcome the arriving guests

Decorate your entrance hall so it offers a warm welcome to arriving guests. Use the living presence of greenery to make your guests sense at once that you are a person who appreciates beauty and enjoys sharing it with his friends.

Luxuriantly tropical plants have an air of opulence that lends easy elegance to a hall or entrance, even though space is limited. Use a massed grouping or a single plant, depending upon the size of entrance hall and other furnishings.

Most plants enjoy a breath of fresh air, but in cold weather you must be sure they aren't exposed to icy blasts each time the front door is opened. Choose the location with this in mind.

Use the most attractive containers you can find, and preserve a polished look by regularly wiping foliage.

If your hall is without windows, plan to move plants to daylight regularly, or provide for adequate artificial lighting.

Foliage creates a flowing line

The leafy grace of large foliage plants set on an insert of tile, marble, or linoleum makes a nice transition from entrance to living room.

Plants with variegated foliage in foreground are two varieties of dieffenbachia; large cutleaf plant next is monstera; at back and as the tallest plants in group are scheffleras.

With plants in pots, you can move them periodically into brighter location for a light bath; to sink or tub for a shower bath.

Plant stands for a formal hall →

Dark green, heart-shaped leaves of *Philodendron cordata* and its willingness to perform in unfavorable light situations make it a universal foliage favorite, deserving of popularity.

As a vining plant it is well suited to display in plant stands such as these, which are of wrought iron, each holding three pots.

Set clay pots in waterproof containers which will protect carpet or floor beneath from damage by water. Dust foliage regularly.

Centerpieces that live and grow

On everyday and special occasions, too, let potted plants decorate your table. Like cut flowers, they make even the simplest of meals seem partylike.

Colorful, flowering plants are an obvious good choice as centerpieces. But don't overlook the decorative potentials of foliage plants. Dress them up with a container to harmonize with the table setting, and you will be surprised at how easily they can take on company manners.

A few pots of English ivy, planted in a silver bowl (give it a protective lining of foil) have the look of classic simplicity which is elegant enough for company, but unpretentious enough for the simplest of meals, when only your family is present. Or make a small dish garden of your favorite foliage plants for a mealtime lift.

Follow the same rules you would for cut flowers, and choose plants that are not so tall that they interfere with across-the-table conversation. Wipe or dust each leaf carefully; pinch off unattractive ones.

Begonias are brighteners

Waxy, pink blooms of the unassuming bedding begonia make lunch or breakfast tables look inviting.

Inexpensive to buy, they will more than pay their way with many weeks of bloom if you shift them to bright light between meals.

Spotlight on clay flowerpots

A famous department store features in its tearoom a dessert served in a red clay flowerpot, echoing the pots of small mums used as centerpiece.

With or without the flowerpot dessert, a group of small flowering plants in their own honest pots makes a new-looking centerpiece. Be sure, of course, that pots are spotlessly clean for such prominent display.

A lusciously pink azalea puts on its pot overcoat of pink for your tea party

Azaleas, in a range of whites, pinks, and reds, are a favorite gift plant at holiday time. Use yours to decorate a party table in attractively feminine fashion.

If you live in a section where the winters are mild, you can set it outdoors where it will grow into a lovely shrub. Keep it moist and out of direct sun when it's blooming indoors.

Foliage and fruit for a party buffet

Husky young dieffenbachia and a line of small, inexpensive peperomias (with the cream and green mottlings) back fruit and candies on a buffet serving table. Use coasters under pots.

After peperomias have served their decorative purpose, repot in larger pots for root growth.

Aluminum plants look stylish

Its silvery leaf markings make inexpensive Aluminum plant (*Pilea cadieri*) pretty enough to bring to the punch table. Wrap pots in lace-paper doilies and back with a blooming azalea plant, if you like.

They'll look new by candlelight

Candlelight and table accessories are to plants what dress-up clothes are to people. Suddenly, they look brand new; you scarcely recognize them in their fresh attire.

You can't arrange plants as you would cut flowers—not without doing them considerable damage through cutting. But you can combine them with candles, set them in an unusual container, get the effect of an arrangement, just as with fresh flowers.

See what an original-looking composition you can create using one of your favorite plants in a new setting. Low-growing ones like African-violets, everblooming begonias, peperomias, dwarf palms, Tri-leaf wonder, are good for the center of the table.

Taller ones such as aspidistras, dieffenbachia, rubber plant, dracaenas, can all be used on buffets, backed with mirrors, and flanked by candles and other appropriate accessories in decorative ways that you design to suit the occasion.

For the holidays, a red-green theme

To decorate a holiday table, set twin pots of Devil's ivy (scindapsus) at each end of a painted white base or long, narrow tray. White mugs are good containers.

Between the two plants, line up a group of low candles—like these, or use the ones that come in their own clear glass cups.

Treat your prettiest African-violet plants to this artistic setting

A hollowed-out piece of driftwood makes a nest for young African-violet plants, with strands of moss to disguise the soil they grow in.

Accompanied by two twisted tapers in a soft green, they're a good illustration of an ingenious and creative way to use house plants as sophisticated table decorations.

Notice how well color harmony between plants and table appointments is developed.

← Use mirror magic to get twice the effect from a plant arrangement

The maranta, or prayerplant, which gets its common name from its habit of folding up its leaves at night, is usually a rather homey and undramatic plant in appearance.

But just see what it does on a linen chest, teamed with brass, red candles, oversize jelly beans, and foil-wrapped chocolates. It says, "Merry Christmas!" to all visitors. Or use other colored accessories for other seasons.

Add your artistry to the natural

Plants displayed with loving artistry can be a constant feature in your home. It will take a little time and ingenuity on your part to select containers and accessories in harmony with plants and setting. But you will have added your personal touch to the natural beauty of the plants in a way that is creative, unique, and satisfying.

Don't think you have to go out and buy everything that goes into your arrangement. Look at familiar household belongings with a fresh eye. A seldom-used tray, fruit bowl, or metal wastebasket may be a handsome accompaniment to plants, and it will have the stamp of freshness and originality.

Another means of letting your taste shine through is with new combinations of plants. Some are far from spectacular by themselves, but together will take on quite a new personality. Coupling sansevieria with pick-a-back plant as on the opposite page is an example of imaginative grouping.

Use accessories with plants to interpret a seasonal theme

What lovelier way is there to express the spirit of Christmas than with small African-violet plants moved from regular shelves to fill a big tray at the feet of a serene Madonna and Child?

beauty of plants

Accessories, such as figurines, candles, driftwood, can give a finished look to the plant arrangement. And they can also help to carry out a holiday or seasonal theme.

But—a word of warning—don't overdo it! If plants are the main feature of your arrangement, use only accessories that advance a theme, are in proper scale. The secret of good paintings—and you are painting a picture with plants—lies in what is left out as well as in what is put in.

Driftwood's a natural with ivy

English ivy, to look its best, wants something to climb on. What's more natural to support the vine, add its own grace to the picture than a lovely, curving branch of driftwood. Help plant get established by securing tips to driftwood with a bit of green florists' tape or yarn.

Contrasting plants paired in a big container make a bold and fresh-looking decoration

Putting two together can multiply your pleasure when you arrange plants for indoor enjoyment. Select two that have built-in contrasts of size, texture, or pattern to complement each other.

Gold-edged sansevieria is never seen to better advantage than when light is shining through its slim, smooth, and marble-patterned leaves.

Cross-light also does much for the hairy pick-a-back plant. Both thrive in less than full sun—in fact, even on a wall opposite from windows.

To get this effect, arrange plants as in sketch—taller one at back, and shorter one front. Fill the watertight outer container with pebbles to hide soil in which plants are growing.

Little gardens that grow in a dish

Fun to plant, pretty to look at are little green gardens that grow in a dish. They're attractive as table centerpieces or decorations for an end table, buffet, or chest.

First, decide where the dish garden is to be placed on display. You'll plant it differently if it's to be viewed from all sides than if it is to be seen mostly from the front.

Select young foliage plants which contrast pleasingly with each other. Include variety of height, leaf shape, size, and patterning. Combine plants that have similar light and water needs so all will have a chance to grow.

Your container may be as simple or as elegant as you like, of metal, ceramic or plastic. But don't have it too shallow. For most plants, at least three inches of depth are needed for stability and for the growth of roots. Provide drainage with a good bottom layer of pebbles, charcoal, or pieces of broken clay pots.

Young plants are glamorous in this mixed planter

Almost any combination of plants can be grouped into a basic triangle—an aesthetically pleasing shape in a shallow container.

Here, tall plant is Chinese evergreen; vine in front of it is "Panamigo," with Hahn's sansevieria backing the variegated peperomia (plant at center and right which shows the most white in its foliage).

Design a long-lasting table decoration of greenery

Spear-like sansevieria planted centrally in a low brass dish is nicely contrasted with the heart-shaped leaves of Philodendron cordatum.

In general, it is most effective to keep the taller plants close together (clumped), tapering to the edges of the container with smaller, low-growing ones; or you can also use vines like the philodendron.

First, choose the spot where the dish garden's to be displayed, then the plants and a container

1 Cover bottom of container with layer of gravel, pebbles, charcoal, or broken clay pots—important since few planters have bottom drainage hole.

Next, add a layer of potting soil. Buy one of special potting mixes available at most garden centers, or mix your own by using equal parts of gravel, garden soil, and peat or compost.

To remove plant from original pot, turn it upside down, place fingers under soil ball, give pot a sharp tap on table edge. The plant should drop out easily.

Place taller plants toward center back in planter to be viewed from front

2 For good looks, and so all plants can be seen, place tall plants in a back and central—or in an off-center—position in the planter.

Once plants are removed from their pots, try not to disturb the roots more than necessary. Remove soil gently as needed to fit plants into the space. Fill in around plants with loose soil only after all are set in place. Then firm the soil with the fingers. Thump container on planting surface once or twice to sift soil about roots. Water well, and your dish garden's ready to place on view!

Lamp table makes a good place to display your dish garden

3 The light boost which a near-by table lamp can give a dish garden helps keep it healthy and growing. All plants used in this one are tolerant of a reduced light situation.

Chinese evergreen is tall plant at center rear; at its left is *Dracaena sanderiana*; at right *Dracaena godseffiana*; in front of it, *Peperomia obtusifolia variegata*. Vine is Devil's ivy.

Chapter 2

Favorite foliage plants

Green is a color you never tire of—restful to the eyes, refreshing to the spirit. That's one reason foliage plants are such perennial favorites. Indoors, in winter, their green leaves hint of summer to come; in summertime, they look cool and woodsy when temperatures soar.

Another reason everyone likes foliage plants is their year-round good looks. Unlike most flowering plants, which favor you with their most beautiful selves for only brief periods, foliage plants are never out of season. They're always ready to decorate the rooms of your home.

You can't possibly grow all the desirable foliage plants there are. Use the pictures and information on the following pages to select those with the qualities you most admire, and which are best suited to the growing conditions that you are able to offer in your home.

All of these foliage plants will thrive in average living room

1. *Kentia palm* is graceful, hardy, and suited to home growing conditions.
2. *Philodendron* with reddish underleaf.
3. *Fiddleleaf fig* leaves look like green polished leather. Makes a tree.
4. *Philodendron* with scalloped leaf edge.
5. *Dieffenbachia picta superba* foliage is a deep green generously splashed with white.
6. *Aralia* leaf outline is like a starburst.
7. *Monstera*, called Philodendron pertusum.
8. *Kangaroo* vine is a pretty trailer.

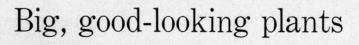

Big, good-looking plants

The luxury look comes easily and quickly to your rooms when you invest in suitable plants of larger size. Or, if time's not important, you can start with young ones, enjoy them as they grow.

Big plants like these need some space around them, and large containers so they'll have a well-balanced, stable appearance. But they make very modest demands so far as daily care is concerned.

All four—rubber plant, fiddleleaf fig next to it, birdsnest fern on the opposite page, and schefflera below—like a filtered or a reflected light, but not full sun. All are large enough to look right spotted on the floor, near wall or window. The fern, especially, asks for below-eye-level placement, so you can see into its rosette-shaped crown.

← *Distinguished trio has big, glossy foliage*

Ficus elastica (get this one by asking for Decora or *Craigi*) does best at temperature of 65° in good light. Grows slowly, seldom requires shifting to a larger pot.

Fiddleleaf fig (*Ficus pandurata*) has same growing needs as rubber plant. Watch both for leaf drop due to poor light, too much water.

Birdsnest fern (*Asplenium nidus*) likes a moist soil, rich in organic materials—peat moss or leaf mold.

Foliage newcomer has deserved popularity

Schefflera isn't a new plant, though its big popularity is fairly recent. It's much in vogue for lobby plantings, and is very decorative.

It has a good green color, rounded outlines, relaxed "hands" of grouped leaflets.

It needs good light but not necessarily sun. Grows somewhat faster than fig or rubber tree. Overwatering will cause bottom leaf drop.

Foliage plants in flower colors will surprise you

If you've always thought of foliage plants as green, you're in for a nice surprise. Gay-as-a-rainbow foliage is not so rare as you may think. Some kinds are seasonal, like fancyleaf caladium that comes in shadings of pink, red, white with green. They grow from tubers indoors in cold weather, in shady garden spots in summer.

Others, like coleus (in low green bowl across the page) are year-arounders. Your florist or greenhouse sells short, bushy plants each spring to set into outdoor flower beds and borders. But you can grow them indoors, too; they're easy to root from stem cuttings. Choose from a riot of reds, yellows, oranges, with or without a mixture of green in their ruffle-edged leaves.

Among other colorful foliage plants not pictured here are begonias (see following pages), velvet plant, calathea, episcia (called Flame-violet), red-nerved fittonia, and some varieties of the vine *tradescantia*.

Caladiums like light but not sun

Start the tubers in wet peat moss or sand. The roots arise from top of tubers, near growing point. After they start, repot; place tubers 1 inch below soil surface. Average-size plants can be grown in from six to eight weeks.

They need warmth and water

Keep caladiums warm. They prefer 70° minimum. Water freely when top growth begins. When the blooming period ends, stop water; rest and dry tubers until next season. Leave in pots, or remove and store in plastic bags.

Splashed with gold, red, and green, the curious croton grows leaves of many different colors on a single plant

Croton plants aren't costly to buy, but neither are they easy to keep growing indefinitely in the home because they need stronger sun, higher humidity than can readily be supplied indoors.

Even though they aren't a long-lasting house plant, you'll enjoy having one around if you regard it as you would cut flowers—discard when faded.

No green thumb needed to grow this hardy, colorful plant

Ever-willing coleus plants can be kept young, short, perky by rooting tips in soil or water when stems get overtall.

Colors are most brilliant when they get regular sunning. If you're displaying this way—out of light—move to a sunny window several times a week.

New variety of an old-time favorite parlor plant is called "Magic Carpet"

Saxifraga sarmentosa is this plant's botanical name. It's also called a strawberry-begonia and strawberry-geranium, although strawberry saxifrage is a more accurate label.

The "strawberry" part of its name comes from its interesting habit of putting out aerial runners, like a garden strawberry, which bear new plantlets at their ends.

New variety shown here is called "Magic Carpet." Old varieties have foliage that is gray-green above and purple below. All like a moist soil, medium light. And all varieties are the easiest of plants to propagate.

For directions on how to have more, see the section on reproduction by runners in the final chapter.

Begonias—among the most beautiful of all

foliage plants—have year-around appeal

Grown more for foliage than for flowers, begonias are among the most satisfying of house plants. Their leaves stay attractive all year long, and if you give them proper light and water, they bloom in winter.

Major classifications of begonias

Tuberous begonias are discussed elsewhere, as are the fibrous-rooted varieties known as "everblooming." Most of those shown here are of the semituberous and rhizomatous types, having a creeping stem, leaves with long hairs. In the Rex group you find purplish leaf backgrounds with silvery surface. Beefsteak begonias (*B. feasti*) have deep red undersides that contrast with smooth, shiny, green tops of their leaves.

Not difficult to grow

Begonias appreciate humid air, but they do not like soil that's constantly moist. Let top soil become dry before you water; then add enough to moisten soil thoroughly.

In winter, they need all the sunlight you can give them; indirect but bright light is best the rest of the year. Foliage becomes pale when sun is too brilliant.

Begonias will tolerate temperature variations, but do best between 65 and 70 degrees.

When potting, set each plant with crown barely above soil, not in depression where water can collect next to the stems. Soil should be light and porous, slightly acid, and contain some peat moss.

← *Handsome trio illustrates wide range of varieties from which to choose*

Rex begonia at left deserves special mention since its hybrids now number in the hundreds and are among the loveliest of house plants. Its heart-shaped leaves are marked, zoned, or spotted with silver, rose, and green.

Smooth-leaved *B. sanguinea* next to it has underleaves the color of red leather. Angelwing displays silver specks on its foliage. Last chapter tells how to multiply any of the plants shown here by means of a leaf cutting.

Leaf types

B. semperflorens flowers

B. semperflorens

B. scandens

B. luxurians

B. heracleifolia

B. lucerna

B. multiflora rosea

B. dregei

B. ricinifolia

B. feasti

B. rex

B. haageana

English ivy and its family
for fascinating foliage patterns

The ivies are surely among the most graceful of vining plants. They're attractive grown in a pot with a trellis or a piece of twisted wood to climb on, or in a low bowl where the tendrils can trail downward. Ivy grows either in water or in soil. The standard English ivy is semi-hardy and can be grown outdoors all winter where weather is relatively mild.

All of the ivies pictured here are varieties of *Hedera helix* (English ivy), *Hedera* being the Latin word for ivy; all are intended primarily for growing indoors, as house plants. There are in existence some 60 to 70 varieties of ivy descended from English ivy, though not more than a score are widely grown for commercial sale by florists and greenhouses.

Ivy prospers in the right surroundings

Bright light, if not direct sun, is necessary for continued growth and health. A common reason for failure is poor light which causes leaf drop and, finally, the end of growth. If its regular location is dimly lighted, move your ivy plant into the sun occasionally to prolong its life.

Use a well-drained soil, rich in organic matter. (The standard potting mixture recommended in Chapter V will be good.) Do not allow the soil to become severely dry, but do not overwater. Best growth results when soil is slightly moist at all times, and temperatures stay within the 50 to 70 degree range.

Root stem cuttings to get new plants

To start a new ivy plant, cut off a stem end 4 or 5 inches long. Remove a few bottom leaves and insert in water, sand,

English ivy

Parent vine from which horticulturists have developed many varieties of less hardy character.

Sylvanian Beauty

Leaves are somewhat smaller than standard English ivy, and much more closely spaced. Distinctive in looks due to its prominent veins.

vermiculite, or perlite. In a few weeks, roots will have grown big enough so cutting may be transferred to standard potting mixture. Best time to make cuttings is spring and summer.

Take your choice of a host of varieties

Among the more popular varieties, in addition to those shown, is Maple Queen. Quite similar in appearance to Sylvanian Beauty pictured opposite, it has full, waxy foliage rather prominently veined. Self-branching, it grows slowly.

For ivies with small, crinkly foliage, choose *H. cordata* (at right), *H. cristata*, or Curlilocks. Manda's crested ivy has a larger leaf than these, grows in bushy shape and when mature, vines out attractively on reddish stems.

H. conglomerata, or Japanese ivy, grows very slowly and is often used in dish gardens because of its upright growth habit, small and closely spaced foliage on a woody stem, which make it resemble a very old vine in miniature.

For something different, the variegated ivies

Glacier ivy, from California, is one of the handsomest of the variegated ivies. Its leaves are an unusual shade of gray-green, nicely marked with white. Gold Dust ivy has golden-yellow mottlings on its dark green leaves.

Widely known is the Variegated Canary Islands ivy (*H. canariensis variegata*), with cream-colored leaves having gray-green areas in the center portion. An effective indoor ivy, it is better adapted than most to hot, dry atmospheres, and one of the showiest of vines to grow in a moss-stick planting.

Suggested uses for ivy as a house plant

Include ivy in a dish garden, for contrast with tall plants. Combine it with bright, red geraniums in a planter that just fits your kitchen window ledge. Grow it in water in a dark green or amber bottle that disguises roots. Set pots in a basket with a handle to serve as a trellis. Or train it to climb on a moss-stick support to any height you like.

Weber's California

One of the daintier of ivy varieties, this one is appealing in a dish garden or in a terrarium to obtain the effect of a miniature.

Cordata

A long-time favorite, *H. helix cordata* is liked for its heart-shaped leaves, with softly rounded contours, compact growth habits.

Hahn's Self-branching

This horticultural variety is notable for its habit of sending out side branches freely, giving it a full and bushy appearance.

Emerald Gem has leaves
that look like arrowheads

Nephthytis, common name of the plant group to which this creeper belongs, is easy to grow. It likes ordinary house temperatures, 65 to 75 degrees, can tolerate low light. Eventually, it gets stringy-looking if grown too long in a dark spot.

Give these plants well-drained soil high in organic matter; or use peat alone and get good results. A moist soil is preferred, but plants get soft if they're overwatered.

White-veined Fittonia
needs light and humidity

Not a rugged plant, Fittonia's lacy veining is so attractive you may be willing to pamper it just because you like its looks. Its scientific name: *Fittonia verschaffelti argyroneura.* It has an equally pretty relative, Red-veined Fittonia, that has the same kinds of cultural needs.

To provide the humid air that's a must, keep a clear plastic cake cover over the plant most of the time—or grow it in a terrarium.

Foursome of vining and trailing plants

To show off the vining and trailing plants to best advantage, place them where the softening effects of their natural growth patterns look appropriate, suited to the location. On tables, window ledges, shelves, in plant boxes, they can spill gracefully over the edge, follow their normal inclinations.

The *syngoniums* (Emerald Gem, shown here, is but one of a big plant group) are well adapted to a moss stick planting. Pickaback plant makes a fine partner for more upright plants in a dish garden. In an indoor planting where you want background greenery, train a grape-ivy to climb a trellis.

A *wicker breadbasket can serve as a plant container*

One of the few popular house plants which is actually native to North America, the Pickaback plant (*Tolmiea menziesia*) ranks among the hardier trailers.

A major attraction is its curious habit of putting out new plants at the base of old leaves — thus its popular name.

To have more, peg young plant to soil in a small pot placed nearby until it roots; cut free and you have a new plant.

Pickaback plant grows best in bright light or sun, and in a uniformly moist soil.

BREADBASKET

SAUCER

Easier to grow than a true ivy, this vine will climb on stake or trellis

Grape-ivy gets its common name from grape-like tendrils by which it can cling to any support you give it. Botanically, it's a *Cissus rhombifolia,* and related to the Kangaroo vine which it resembles.

It requires a light, well-drained soil, does best in filtered sunlight. Don't overwater; allow surface soil to become dry before adding water. It prefers a room temperature of from 55 to 65 degrees.

Readily propagated from cuttings, this is one of the most satisfactory vines for indoor use. Tolerates low light and humidity better than true ivies. You'll like it in an indoor planter or in a dish garden.

Appeal of a vine depends on how and where it's used

Vining plants can hold their own with the most aristocratic of house plants if they have the right setting and container.

Always useful in combination with bigger or upright-growing specimens in an indoor planter, vines needn't always take a back seat. Use a little imagination in the way you show them off, and vines alone can do an impressive job of decoration.

Vines that complement each other

In a wall planter, try a combination of vines that add to each other's looks. Here, Canary Islands Ivy, Devil's ivy with variegated foliage look better for the addition of philodendron.

English ivy's right in a masculine setting

Any one of many English ivy varieties would lend itself to this treatment—combined with wooden decoy and handsome pewter plate, shown against a wood-paneled wall. To keep the ivy growing luxuriantly, you must supply bright light and adequate moisture. Shelf placement makes the most of an ivy's natural habit of growth, gives it an edge over which to trail its curving stems.

New container for an old favorite among vines

Because it's so easy to grow, so widely grown, it's easy to take the Heartleaf philodendron for granted as a house plant.

But give it a polished brass mortar and pestle set as a container, and suddenly it's as elegant a small and shapely vine as you could wish for.

Philodendron cordatum—like all philodendrons—does best in a moist soil; withstands a low light situation, but grows more luxuriantly in medium light. It will grow in water, but leaves may become too widely spaced.

Dramatic leaf pattern of Canary Islands variegated ivy suits this moss-stick planting

Isn't this a dramatic way to display a vine? Creamy-white leaf markings of a variegated Canary Islands ivy plant show off to maximum advantage against a plain background. Good design of ceramic jardiniere makes its contribution to the effect.

This is not one of the easy-to-grow house plants, but it does repay you for extra effort with its elegant appearance.

Canary Islands ivy needs a brightly lighted or sunny location if it is to grow well.

It also demands more humidity than is ordinarily available indoors in wintertime. You can supplement humidity by keeping the moss stick on which it is growing constantly moist, and by frequently spraying the foliage with tepid water. Take it to the sink for this operation!

The decorative monsteras and philodendrons

Ever-increasing assortment
of philodendrons offers
beautiful and durable foliage

The collection of philodendrons pictured at left is but a sample of the variety of leaf shapes and sizes included in the philodendron family.

Shown with them is their close ally, *Monstera deliciosa*, often sold as cutleaf philodendron, and called a Swiss Cheese plant because of the holes that perforate the large split leaves next to the central rib. Monstera has much the same needs as the philodendrons.

Natives of the tropical jungles of Central and South America, the philodendrons have become the most popular of indoor foliage plants.

Monstera is a favorite of
decorators because of
its sophisticated appearance

For modern interiors that depend on solid colors and the sweep of plain, undecorated surfaces to achieve major effects, the big, deeply split leaves of monstera can often add just a proper amount of contrasting pattern.

The several varieties of monstera require somewhat brighter light than philodendrons, or the leaves will not split to the extent that they should.

In all other requirements, monstera is like the philodendrons and wants a loose, porous soil; sufficient water to keep soil moist, not wet; average temperatures of from 65 to 75 degrees.

In a dish garden, try combining monstera and heartleaf philodendron

Young plants of monstera often have leaves that are entire or show only a few splits. As the plant grows older, if given the right light and moisture, it puts out larger leaves which are much more profusely slit.

Heartleaf philodendron (*P. cordatum*) also varies greatly in size and spacing of its foliage depending on the conditions under which it is grown.

If grown over a period of time in poor light and low humidity, this vine becomes stringy, puny, and new leaves are smaller and smaller. To start a new vine, take a sturdy tip cutting and root.

Only ordinary care is needed to keep this fine threesome growing

Philodendron varieties shown, left to right, are: *P. dubia, P. panduriforme, P. hastatum.*

Of the three, panduriforme is probably best suited to growing on a moss stick, since it has the strongest vining tendency. Also called a fiddle-leaf philodendron for its 3-lobed foliage, it grows more rapidly than the larger leaved varieties do.

Philodendron dubia is one of the most reliable of the fernlike varieties. Others which resemble it are *P. laciniosum, P. selloum,* and *P. elegans,* all deeply lobed.

Other philodendrons having a shield-shaped leaf, something like *hastatum,* include: *mandaianum, erubescens* (reddish cast to foliage), *sodiroi* (mottled light gray on an olive-green leaf).

Make your own moss sticks

*It's easy to make
a cylinder for a
moss stick planting of
your favorite vine*

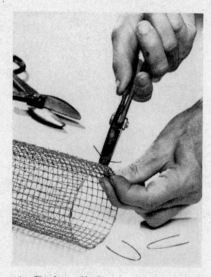

1 Basic cylinder is made of ¼-inch hardware cloth. Buy a 10-inch strip, either 30 or 36 inches wide, depending on how tall you want the planting to be when finished.

Roll cloth into cylinder. Overlap edges about ¾ of an inch; fasten at 6-inch intervals with strands of wire. Cut off surplus wire.

Gold-splashed Devil's ivy (*Scindapsus*) is the vine used for this planting. It needs humidity and bright light to thrive. For dimly lighted spot, try philodendron instead.

2 Put an inch or two of gravel in tub for drainage. Push two small sticks through bottom of cylinder as shown, to help brace it. Flat sticks are best, can be slipped in if wire is cut slightly. Fill about cylinder with standard potting soil mixture.

3 Make mixture of half peat moss, half vermiculite or perlite. To get mixture properly damp, soak peat moss overnight beforehand.

Paper funnel is a help in filling. Stop at intervals as you fill and tamp mixture down with broom handle.

4 Space vines about pole in tub—3 to 5 for a planting of size pictured.

Fill around roots with soil to within an inch of rim to allow room for watering. Use any favorite vine.

Care after planting

Train by twisting vines to grow in spiral around pole. Fasten the vines to the pole with hairpins inserted at a sharp angle.

Push a small pot into cylinder top and fill with water. It will seep down into pole, provide a moist medium for support roots to grow into. Add water daily.

When you water, fill tub to the brim; let water settle. Repeat until it drains out at bottom, then empty saucer. Let surface soil get dry before re-watering.

Another kind of moss stick

Choose a stake no longer than 2 feet. Spread a pound of dampened sphagnum moss on paper, as shown. To start, roll edge of paper with moss for a half-turn. Press firm as you roll.

*Use rustproof wire
to hold sphagnum moss
on wood plant stake*

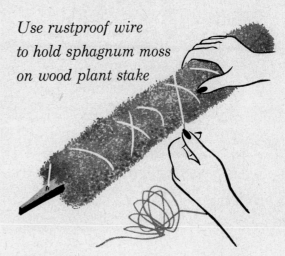

Fasten wire at bottom of stake; wind spirally upward, with turns about 2 inches apart. Adjust moss to cover top of stake; wind spirally down to base and fasten. If moss stick looks ragged, wrap tightly in paper for 15 minutes.

Insert moss stick in pot firmly. Plant the vines at its base. To help them get established, fasten tips to moss stick with hairpins or staples.

For success with a planting of this type, the moss stick must be kept constantly moist.

Striking foliage

These plants—some common,

If your home is small and space for plants limited, this group will interest you.

None of the plants shown grows large under average home conditions, though *syngonium* (left) can be trained to climb a moss stick. All have intriguing foliage that is remarkable for pattern or for shape.

←

Divided leaves of a rich, dark green

Syngonium podophyllum auritum or "Five Fingers," is the name of this dainty climber. Grown in a pot, it would resemble the Trileaf Wonder, also a *syngonium*, pictured opposite. Young plants are upright, vining as they mature.

Explore the peperomias if you like your plants small and dramatic

All peperomias like medium light and warm temperatures—not below 65 degrees at night. Grow in porous soil and do not overwater.

Varieties pictured are Emerald Ripple, at each end of planter; *P. obtusifolia variegata*, showing a good deal of white in its foliage; a vining type at front; solid green *P. obtusifolia* at rear; *P. sandersii*, or Watermelon peperomia, named for silvery markings on leaves.

patterns make these worth a second look

some rare—will grow slowly, take only a limited amount of space

Trileaf Wonder has cream-tinted foliage

Trileaf Wonder, a patented *Syngonium podophyllum*, is an easy-to-grow plant that will tolerate low light. Grow in a loose loam or peat moss.

Aphelandra sports a patent-leather gloss

This highly distinctive plant needs sun and high humidity if it is to thrive. Aphelandra, if grown under glass, produces spikes of highly showy bloom.

Star-shape marks Norfolk Island Pine

Grow in sunlight and syringe needle-like foliage frequently as a means of increasing the humidity. Botanically, it is an *Araucaria excelsa*.

Dainty trailer that blooms in winter

Ornamental foliage of Ruellia makes it a desirable plant all year round. If it receives enough humidity, produces lavender blooms in winter.

Velvety foliage is distinctively colored

Foliage of purplish cast has strong veinings of a pink tone. The Chamaeranthemum is ideal to grow in a terrarium because it likes high humidity.

Trio of dracaenas in a corner grouping

Largest plant, at rear, is *Dracaena fragrans massangeana*, also called the Corn Plant. In foreground are two specimens of *D. deremensis warneckii*, sharply striped with white and gray. Once established, plants are long-lived.

Smaller varieties make good centerpieces

Dracaena godseffiana is quite unlike the other members of its family in appearance, having yellow-dotted glossy green leaves on wiry stems. Little *D. sanderiana* has two white bands bordering a gray-green central stripe.

Dracaena

A number of interesting

Common striped dracaena has so often been relegated to the background of a large indoor planting that it acquires a fresh and unusual air when brought out of its corner and shown as an independent plant.

Smaller dracaenas, too, have enough character to warrant their more frequent use as single plants, attractive in their own right. *D. godseffiana* and *D. sanderiana*, both of which are pictured below, are among the best of the dwarf-growing types.

Regardless of size, dracaenas in general thrive on damp soil, providing drainage is good and temperatures fairly high—not dropping below 65 degrees at night. As to light requirements, they do well either in bright or in medium light.

If leaf tips become brown, it is usually a sign of improper watering. Too little or too much water will produce that condition.

→

Handle it properly and dracaena's at home in the most polished setting

One of the commonest varieties of dracaena, *D. massangeana* will win enthusiastic praise if you dress it up with an attractive cover, set it down where it can be admired from all sides. Do take precautions against water marks (see sketch and suggestions below), or set pot into a glazed ceramic jardiniere.

Closely related to this favorite are such horticultural varieties as *D. victoria* and *D. lindenii*. Other recommended varieties include *D. draco* and *D. marginata*, a red-edged type which is a native of Madagascar.

ELASTIC POT COVER
OF STRAW

POT

ALUMINUM FOIL
TO PREVENT LEAKAGE

WOOD BLOCK

—a versatile plant that merits attention

species have leaves that are long and broad, striped in white or yellow

Palms to add an air of elegance

Palms and elegance have a natural affinity. When informality was the dominant decorative motif, potted palms were out of style. Now that a return to elegance is a noticeable decorating trend, palms are in vogue.

Of the palms small enough to be suitable for growing indoors, the most popular are *Howea belmoreana* (Kentia), the miniature date palm from India, *Phoenix roebeleni*, and the slender *Chamaedorea elegans*.

An undemanding house plant

Palms grow so slowly indoors that they may be kept in the same pot for years by unpotting and removing about one-fourth of the root system each year. They prefer a container that seems small in proportion to their over-all size and height.

This means water requirements must be checked frequently. Palms should not dry out completely. If this happens, plunge pot in water; leave until soil is saturated.

Use palms as a centerpiece

Sold under various trade names, young palm plants are often used in dish gardens. Try planting three in a sophisticated container to use as a long-lasting table decoration.

In a container like this, put in a layer of pebbles first, to supply bottom drainage.

Kentia palm suits an interior decorated in a modern manner

Nice embellishment for a refined, modern room is a Kentia palm in a gleaming brass outer container, attractive in itself and serving the utilitarian purpose of protecting the floor from water stains.

Palms need warmth (minimum night temperature of 60 degrees), moist soil, and bright light. Set them in the sun occasionally if the regular location is dimly lighted.

Leaf ends look like a tuna tail

Still a palm, but looking quite different from the feather-leaved varieties is this *Chamaedorea geonomiformis*. Each big leaf is split at the end so that it resembles a tuna tail. Prominent veining adds further interest to its unusual foliage.

The trunk is single, and mature leaves grow to be as much as a foot in length.

One of the favorite parlor palms

Neanthe bella (*Chamaedorea elegans*) is a slender palm that grows tall without being very wide or spreading. Tolerates dry air, but needs to have soil kept moist.

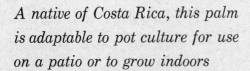

A native of Costa Rica, this palm is adaptable to pot culture for use on a patio or to grow indoors

With the increasing popularity of palms, a great many new varieties are constantly being imported from Central and South America. This one, *Chamaedorea costaricana*, has the habit of growing in clumps, like bamboo.

Major potential source of trouble with this, as with all palms grown indoors, is water. If dead leaves develop, this is an almost certain indication of too little; if dead spots appear on single leaves, it is probably a sign that the plant is getting too bright sun and too little water.

Among the possible pests that may attack the palms, mealy bugs, redspider-mites, and scale insects are the main ones to watch for.

Ferns need bright light and a rich loam

←

*Place ferns where passersby
won't rub against delicate fronds*

Birdsnest Fern (*Asplenium nidus*), native
of Brazil, puts out a whorl of fronds of
spatula shape which grow to two feet or
more in length. It is most attractive as a
house plant when it is young.

To thrive, ferns need filtered sunlight.
Grow them in soil that is rich in organic
matter—50 per cent or more of peat. A
moist but well-drained soil is best.

→

*For that fresh and lacy look,
you'll choose the Boston Fern*

The Boston Fern (*Nephrolepis*) and its
numerous varieties wear spring's tender
green all year long. Mass them like this to
give any room a lift.

The mature plants put out runners from
which it is possible to propagate a new
fern. When an older fern has become pot-
bound, unpot and separate the root mass
carefully into two or more plants.

←

*An old-fashioned-looking fern
that has returned to popularity*

Whitman, Curly, Crested, Ostrich-plume
— these are some of the names by which
the more finely divided varieties of the
common Boston Fern are known.

As natives of tropical regions, ferns dislike cold. They grow best at a minimum
temperature of 65 degrees. In wintertime,
set ferns back from windows so that frond
ends do not touch the cold glass.

No pampering is asked by these foliage toughies

This one grows where nothing else will

For durability under the least favorable of conditions, the Aspidistra or cast-iron plant is hard to equal. Grows best in an out-of-the-sun location.

A less exacting group of plants than the collection shown here would be hard to find. They can withstand almost any indoor adversity except overwatering. They will continue to grow in hot, dry, or conditioned air.

Except for the screwpine, which does need some filtered sunlight, they have the ability to survive in quite dim corners.

Give these plants a porous soil, adequate drainage, water them sparingly and they'll live for years. For appearances' sake, dust them occasionally with a dampened cloth so that their somewhat leathery foliage will be at its polished, glossy best.

Members of the succulent family, the sansevierias need very little water

The tall variety is S. *trifasciata zeylanica;* rosette is a new sport of familiar dark green S. *hahni.* This one is called Golden Hahni, after the two gold bands that run the length of each leaf. Use sansevierias in planters and dish gardens, but don't combine them with plants which need large amounts of water.

Striped Bowstring Hemp's a favorite

Botanically, it's S. *trifasciata laurenti*. Planted with heartleaf philodendron, it grows nicely in low light. It's a good choice to decorate a man's office.

The rubber plant grows to tree size

Variegated Indian Rubber plant, *Ficus elastica variegata*, makes a handsome room decoration, withstands neglect, lack of sunlight. Do not overwater.

Sample the less common sansevierias

S. *liberica* is striped with white; S. *parva* is low-growing, with narrow, curved leaves; S. *cylindrica* (shown in flower) has curious, tube-like foliage.

Sword-like leaves have spiny margins

Pandanus or screwpine thrives in warm indoor temperatures. Water moderately in summer; keep definitely on dry side in winter. It needs filtered sunlight.

Dieffenbachias flourish
in locations receiving filtered light

Dieffenbachias are big, luxuriant plants that catch and hold attention in any room setting which allows them space to spread out their decorative foliage.

There are some 20 varieties of the plant in cultivation, most having dark green foliage with creamy white or pale chartreuse markings or variegations.

A common name for the plant (its botanical name honors German physician and botanist J. F. Dieffenbach) is Dumb Cane. It is so called because those who chew it temporarily lose the power of speech. Under no circumstances should any portion of the plant be placed in the mouth.

The dieffenbachia grows best in a well-drained soil rich in organic matter: half garden loam, half peat would be a good mixture. Although it will stay alive and grow slowly in very dim locations, it needs some filtered light if it is to prosper.

When grown in poor light, the plant's natural tendency to become "leggy" is greatly increased. When bare stem becomes too long, use the process of air layering, explained in last chapter, to re-root the plant.

←

This variety is generously splashed with chartreuse

If chartreuse would be a good accent in your color scheme, you'll like this horticultural variety of the dieffenbachia—Rudolph Roehrs.

As for all dieffenbachias, keep the soil in which it is growing uniformly moist, but not wet.

Grow it either as a single specimen or in combination with other plants in an indoor planter.

→

Other varieties have white feathering on green foliage

All dieffenbachia varieties known as *picta* (which means "painted") show greater or smaller amounts of white patterning or veining.

Among the recommended ones are *D. picta memoria, D. picta bausei. Dieffenbachia amoena* also displays white markings, but is so large a plant that it should be used only where there is space for growth.

Bromeliads worth growing
for exotic bloom, ornamental foliage

A delightfully bizarre group of plants, the bromeliads have long starred in botanical garden exhibits, attracting attention with their brilliant blooms and neat rosettes of foliage, often so shiny it looks varnished.

Many can really be classed as succulents since they often store an emergency supply of water, not inside fleshy leaves as succulents do, but within a natural vase-shaped center formed by their durable foliage.

Natives of the tropical forests of Central and South America, bromeliads fall into two distinct groups: terrestrials, which grow in soil or between rocks; epiphytes, which are tree-dwellers. In the second group, many can exist for long periods without roots, so long as they receive moisture from reservoirs located in their leaf bases.

In spite of exotic looks and growth habits, many bromeliads are easy to grow. The main requirement is that the growing medium (osmunda fern root fiber is recommended) be kept constantly moist; cups at leaf bases should be filled at each watering.

They're members of the pineapple family

At left, aechmea hybrid (Fosters Favorite) has wine-red foliage; center plant is of cryptanthus species; at right is *Cryptanthus fosterianus*. All of these bromeliads grow best in filtered sunlight.

For height, show palms with bromeliads

In the background is *Chamaedorea erumpens*, another tropical plant that complements the two bromeliads. At left is a striped cryptanthus hybrid; at right a vriesia hybrid, Mariae, with light green foliage.

In winter come showy spikes of bloom which may remain attractive for several months

Vriesia carinata, at left, is one of the best of bromeliads for decorative use because of its feathered crimson and yellow bracts, pale green foliage.

At center, *Aechmea fulgens discolor* from Brazil produces spikes tipped with violet flowers; later come the red berries that are pictured.

Purple-flowered *Tillandsia lindeni*, though you'd scarcely recognize it as such, is a close relative of Spanish moss which drapes itself on trees and wires through the Deep South. From Peru, this is one of the rarer of the bromeliads shown here.

Almost the only house-plant pest to attack the bromeliads is leaf scale. Usually, it can be successfully eliminated by sponging foliage with warm, soapy water; rinse with clear water.

Set tree-dwelling bromeliads on a curving wooden branch to imitate the natural habitat

To sharpen the naturally spectacular character of these odd plants, set them growing on a "bromeliad tree."

Wash soil gently from roots; wrap in pre-dampened osmunda fiber. Use fine wire to secure moss about roots and to fasten plant to tree branch. When watering, use a spray bulb to moisten moss; also fill the natural cups at leaf bases with water.

Growing in the large pot at the base of the bromeliad tree is *Vriesia splendens;* perched just above it is a vriesia hybrid, Mariae; higher on the branch is *Tillandsia lindeni;* in smaller pot, a cryptanthus hybrid.

For pot-grown bromeliads, the big danger is rotting off at the base due to excessive moisture. Avoid this by supplying good bottom drainage.

Most varieties of this bromeliad type have foliage mottled with red or maroon

A neoregelia hybrid with its richly mottled color comes as close as any plant can to being a bit of living statuary. Blooms are fiery-red bells.

Neoregelia spectabilis, a popular variety of this bromeliad, has metallic green leaves that end in pronounced tips of contrasting blood red and account for its common name of Painted Fingernail plant.

Endless variety recommends the bromeliads to a collector

In or out of bloom, the bromeliads are collectors' items. At first glance, they seem much alike in their typically rosette shapes. But a closer look reveals striking variations in the artful designs with which nature has endowed them.

Remarkable for their beautiful leaf designs and brilliant flower spikes, they are also easy to grow and maintain. Although they will continue to live in dim light, they need filtered sunlight if they are to flower indoors. Occasional feeding with organic fertilizer is beneficial.

→

Three green and growing beauties to lift your spirits on a dull day

Vriesia fenestralis (left) has a distinctive dense whorl of broad foliage decorated with a network of fine darker green lines.

Accompanying it are *Nidularium innocentii lineatum*, its lettuce-green leaves striped with ivory; and (foreground) another member of the vriesia group.

Pebble mulch in pots is good looking and practical since it serves to lessen evaporation from porous growing medium.

←

Unexpected colorings and forms have the look of man-made art

Billbergias, of which this is an example, are among the most frequently encountered and fastest growing of the bromeliads.

The easiest method of propagation is by means of division. Small offshoot you see at left of the parent plant can be removed, potted separately. It will produce its own bloom by the following year.

Cactus plants belong to the big succulent family

All cactus plants are succulents, though the reverse is not true. There are nearly 30 separate groups of plants that include varieties which are succulents, the cactus being but one of the tribe. And since it is not always easy to be certain which of the thorny and prickly plants is a true cactus, it is safest to refer to all plants in the group with the general term "succulents."

Succulence in a plant means the ability to store water. Among the succulents are some of the most highly varied and remarkably well adapted plants in the world—able to exist on high mountains, in deserts, on the seashore, and in tropical jungles.

This genius for survival in unfavorable locations is due to their cell structure, as shown in the diagram opposite. Once you know how they are made, your success with the succulents will be more certain, for you will understand their special requirements concerning heat, light, soil, and water.

Vegetable camels, the succulents are 90 per cent water. See how they are able to pipe and store it:

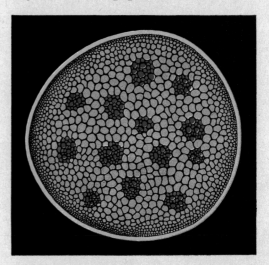

Slightly waxy outer skin, almost impervious to water and gases covers leaves, stems as shown in this much-enlarged cross section of a stem.

Small, hard-walled cells inside skin are a barrier to escape of water from big, thin-walled cells that are inner reservoirs of food, water.

Scattered throughout mass of inner cells are water tubes, several to a bundle. They conduct water taken in by roots up through the plant

Specialized tubes carrying food run alongside water tubes but conduct in both directions, letting succulents live on reserves between rains.

Dish garden of cactus and succulents →

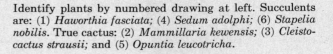

Identify plants by numbered drawing at left. Succulents are: (1) *Haworthia fasciata;* (4) *Sedum adolphi;* (6) *Stapelia nobilis.* **True cactus:** (2) *Mammillaria kewensis;* (3) *Cleistocactus strausii;* and (5) *Opuntia leucotricha.*

Comes from Somaliland

Kalanchoe somaliensis has attractive glossy leaves, with saw-toothed margins. Mature plant is about 1 foot tall.

Living, growing

Euphorbia pedilanthus tithymaloides

Echeveria secunda   *Sedum pachyphyllum*   *Sedum adolphi*

Jadeplant has a tree-like shape

Crassula argentea (botanical name of this popular succulent) branches, and grows old beautifully. This one's over a foot tall; some grow to 3 feet or taller as potted plants.

Succulent dish garden's exotic

Crassula arborescens is tall plant at back; leaning out at right is *Crassula perforata* (String o' Buttons); *Sedum adolphi* and *Echeveria* are low, rosette shapes in front.

plants that look like works of art

Bryophyllum pinnatum

Succulent plants take so many fascinating shapes and forms, and so many of them have dwarf or small growth patterns that they make ideal house plants. Their sculptured looks ask for unusual containers. Shallow bowls and dishes make fine sites for desert scenes featuring an assortment of your favorites.

Planting and care are easy—providing you can give succulents good sun and the right amount of water. Resist temptation to overwater, for this will quickly produce rot. Wait, always, until soil is dry to the touch, then water thoroughly, being sure you've provided for adequate bottom drainage.

Equal parts of coarse sand or gravel and garden loam make a good soil—porous enough to drain excess water, yet firm enough to hold the required amount of moisture. Succulents need more water during periods of rapid growth (in summer), less during the winter when plants go into a dormant season.

← Succulents belong to many different plant families

Euphorbia's also called "Devil's spine." *Bryophyllum* produces plantlets on leaf edges; *Echeveria* sends up circle of young plants around mother plant; *Sedum pachyphyllum* leaves turn red in sun; *Sedum adolphi* foliage has a powdery, gray-green color.

So bizarre and intriguing are succulents that fanciers of this family never seem to have all the wanted kinds. But it's easy to grow more to trade with fellow collectors.

Spring and summer are best for taking cuttings, since plants are then in a growing phase and success is surest.

Many succulents grow offsets at soil level. For these, you need only detach offset from mother plant, insert in soil that is half coarse sand, half garden loam. Keep dry a few days; then water as usual.

Make stem and leaf cuttings

Danger of rot is greater for stem or leaf cuttings than for offsets. Guard against it by allowing the cutting to dry off for a few days in a cool, shaded spot.

When wound has "healed over," plant cutting in damp—not wet—sand. Leave it there, watering sparingly until it has taken root before transplanting to usual sand and loam mixture. Cuttings handled this way should root in a few weeks.

Pair off contrasting varieties

Here are two curious succulents to silhouette against a plain wall: metallic-colored rosettes of echeverias, and the lanky euphorbias which discourage familiarities by means of their armor of make-believe thorns.

Set a succulent dish garden outdoors

Both crassulas and echeverias grow in the rosette shapes which predominate in this succulent dish garden. The tall blooms at the back are of the kalanchoe. Plants that look like clusters of beads are of the sedum group.

Among the best of aloes

Aloe arborescens is well known and much cultivated for its statuesque lines. In its native habitat, it grows to a height of 15 feet. Has red flowers at end of winter.

endless variety of size and shape

Strong leaf patterns give this variety
its common name of partridge breast

Another much-sought-after succulent is this *Aloe variegata*. It grows in rosettes which are triangular in shape, its leaves edged and marbled sharply with white on dark green.

If succulents interest you, the aloes are worth getting to know. Botanists have identified more than 200 varieties ranging in size from 3 or 4 inches to trees of 30 to 40 feet in height.

Fascinating foliage makes this
kalanchoe a good potted plant

Brown-pointed markings on its leaves make the *Kalanchoe tomentosa*, or panda plant, as it's commonly called, pretty to grow as a house plant. As it grows older, it puts out side branches from a central stem in a bushy growth pattern.

Scientific species name (*tomentosa*) indicates that its leaves are entirely covered with dense matting of hairs, giving it a furry look.

Here's a plant chameleon which lives
up to its common name of stoneface

Lithops loucheana, as this odd little succulent is called, is much like all other lithops except for upper markings by which one variety is distinguished from the 50-some other members of the family—all native to South Africa.

The plant consists of leaves in pairs, split by a central fissure from which flowers emerge. The lithops customarily grow in clumps, as here.

Cotyledon has leaves that curve upward
like cups to catch the rain or dew

Cotelydon undulata is a pretty, bushy variety of succulent, with wavy edges on up-curved leaves, which are covered with a thick, waxy pure-white bloom that rubs off when the plant is handled. A mature plant reaches a height of 3 feet and bears orange-colored blooms during the summer.

The name cotyledon comes from ancient Greek and means a cavity—after cuplike leaves of some varieties, such as this one. Some 30 species have been identified, mostly natives of South Africa.

Chapter 3

Favorite flowering plants

Everyone loves the flowering house plants. Their fresh blooms—sometimes fragrant, always colorful—catch and hold the eye of all who enter the room.

Some flowering plants are in bloom for only brief seasons of the year, others continuously. You can, if you plan it right, have a variety in bloom all year.

On these two pages we present a sampling of the flowering house plants you'll want to get acquainted with if you don't already know them. The pages to follow contain more detailed information on how to grow all of these plus a good many others.

Of the obliging beauties that are perpetually in bloom, everflowering begonia and African-violet head the list. And geraniums will reward you with two long seasons of bloom if you take stem cuttings at the correct time. Cuttings rooted in late summer bring fall and winter blooms in addition to spring and summer flowering.

Others are truly seasonal, to be enjoyed while their brief beauty lasts, then looked forward to for another year. Maybe this enhances their desirability. Would amaryllis or the spring flowering tulips and hyacinths be as enchanting if you could have them in bloom every day and any day?

Seasonal or perpetual, grow these flowering house plants for the gifts of color and freshness they bring to your home.

Blooms all year

African-violets may well be the most widely grown of all house plants. They come in wide color range.

Command an early spring by forcing bulbs

Hyacinths and tulips are favorite spring bulbs to bring into bloom indoors, while winter still holds sway outdoors. Many of the other spring flowering bulbs can also be forced successfully. Or buy them at your florist shop from December on.

Tender amaryllis bulbs will bloom indoors in time for Christmas

Newer, cold-treated amaryllis bulbs take but three weeks or so to come into bloom, just in time for the holiday season.

Their wide, flat faces may be as much as eight inches across, in solid reds, oranges salmon pink, or white—or in those colors, striped with white. The finest bulbs are bigger than teacups, imports from Holland.

Gloxinias in glowing colors are star performers for spring and summer

You can grow gloxinias from tubers, as we show you later on in this chapter. Or, if you have patience, you can develop new tubers from leaf cuttings of a blooming plant.

Once a plant comes into bloom, buds will continue to unfold for weeks. Available colors include white, white-fringed scarlets to a deep indigo, as well as solid red.

The red geranium at the window sill symbolizes the friendly and informal pattern of family living

Geraniums are so inexpensive to buy each spring as bedding plants that you'll have had your money's worth if you just enjoy them while they bloom and then discard.

But you can easily make a rewarding hobby of them, taking cuttings, collecting the varieties with distinctive foliage, blooms of many hues—white, pinks, and reds. See later pages for instructions on methods of making stem cuttings of all varieties.

African-violets are a favorite

To grow still bigger, handsomer specimens has become a national

The African-violet has amazing charm. It isn't really a violet at all, though it comes from Africa. But it grows flowers that look like violets, in violet colors of blue, white, purple, plus soft, heavenly pink, both single and double, as well as ruffled. Foliage, too, differs from one variety to another, with some more glossy, more hairy, or more quilted looking than others.

Saintpaulias, to use the correct botanical name, keep on blooming for months on end, and are among the easiest of all house plants to propagate. If you join the African Violet Society, you'll soon be trading leaves with collectors the country over to increase your treasury of varieties.

There *are* some tricks to growing handsome African-violets. Learn what they are in the pages that follow. Light, water, feeding, you'll find, are the big three keys to success.

Blue Warrior naturally grows into a nosegay

Scores of new varieties of African-violets have been developed over the past decade or so. This one, Blue Warrior, is particularly attractive because of its habit of putting up all the blooms at the center, like a carefully arranged nosegay.

African-violets will grow under artificial light

house plant in millions of households

game. Grow a few, and you'll soon boast like a veteran

Good, strong electric light actually substitutes for daylight with African-violets. See section on growing plants under artificial light for more detailed information on this method of cultivation. The clear lavender-blues, rosy pinks, bicolors, frost-crystal whites, and deep reddish purples provide you with an endless variety of bloom. A big collection like this looks its best seen from above; display on low table.

*African-violets like
an even temperature
and light soil mixture*

Wayzata variety pictured, like all African-violets, prefers temperature of 70° to 72°. When house temperature drops below 60°, the growth is slowed down.

Since these temperatures are average home temperatures, few precautions are necessary. On a very cold night, it's advisable to give some protection to a plant on a window sill by lowering blind, placing heavy cardboard between the plant and window glass.

Best soil mixture is one-third each of garden loam, coarse sand, and of humus, leaf mold, or peat moss.

Follow these tips for better plants

*They'll star for you
if you give them
proper light and water*

An east or west window is usually best for African-violets, as direct rays of south sun may burn leaves. North window, except during summer, probably does not supply adequate light.

Or grow under artificial light. See section on this subject in Chapter five for more detailed information.

Water when top soil feels dry, or use wick-type container. Use room temperature water. Very cold water, straight from tap, will spot leaves if it gets on them.

*These fastidious little
plants repay you
for good care with
constant succession
of colorful bloom
the whole year around*

In shifting, potting, or repotting, you can keep plants free of soil by using a funnel. Make one of paper, if you like, and spoon the soil into it. Have the potting soil damp; water well immediately afterward.

For prize-winning plants, you want only a single crown. Use a sharp knife to detach competing growth, usually before it has reached this size. The portion you've cut loose can be rooted to produce new plant.

Mealy bugs do sometimes attack an African-violet plant. Eliminate them with nail-polish remover on cotton swab. Touch each white dot. Repeat the treatment every third day as long as necessary.

African-violets *do* like an occasional shower bath. The only harm that can result is due not to the water getting onto leaves, but to using water that is too cold. Use fine spray of lukewarm water.

Dust foliage frequently, but be gentle about it. Use a discarded leaf, a brush with soft bristles, or a pipe cleaner to do the job. Stroke from leaf base to tip — with the furry nap of the foliage.

Wick-style containers work well for African-violets, since they keep soil uniformly moist, and require little attention from you. Have water lukewarm; add plant food to water as package directs.

Smooth edge of ceramic pot's ideal for African-violets. If using an unglazed clay pot, cover edge with cellophane tape, dip in paraffin, or shellac to protect leaves from harmful salts pot soaks up.

Use sharp knife to sever a leaf from mother plant, with 1- to 2-inch stem attached. Choose leaf with a firm, not a rubbery stem.

Here's all you'll need to know about multiplying your African-violets

It's so easy to have more of your favorite African-violets that you may have to resist a temptation to grow too many. But they do make fine gifts, and if you become a collector, of course you'll want to raise young plants to trade for new varieties.

Leaves will root in water or sand

A healthy leaf from a mother plant will root in water, although water-produced roots are less vigorous than those grown in sand, vermiculite, or perlite and may suffer greater setback when transferred from water to potting soil. To learn how to do it either way, see the pictures and instructions along the margins of these pages.

Tips on potting your young plants

Whether you've rooted your leaves in water, vermiculite, perlite, or sand, the same advice about potting a young plant applies: select a small pot to start with—a two- or three-inch pot at most. Young plants in too big a pot are difficult to water properly since roots fill so small a proportion of total soil ball, and it may be dry on the surface while still quite damp at the center. As the plant grows, shift it to a pot of the next larger size.

Not essential, but an extra insurance of vigorous roots is the step of dipping stem end into a root-promoting powder.

Insert treated leaves in moistened vermiculite or a coarse sand to root. Use a small pot if rooting only one or two leaves.

If you want to start many leaves at a time, use a cake pan filled with a rooting media. Sprinkle with lukewarm water to moisten to bottom of container. Plastic cover traps moist air.

To root leaves in water, cover a jar with foil or wax paper; punch holes in top and insert leaves. They will root in 2 to 4 weeks. Then pot in a sandy soil until new leaves appear.

This is an attractive way to display an African-violet that's also good for the plant

Although African-violets can tolerate rather dry air, they prefer high humidity. Here's a way to provide it, while also displaying the plant to good advantage, and reducing your need to water it so often.

Line bottom of large glass or plastic globe with a 2-inch layer of sphagnum moss; lower plant carefully into bowl; tuck in extra moss to hide pot. Keep moss damp so it will, by gradual evaporation, moisten air inside of the globe.

Because they like humidity, young African-violet plants are good to include with others in a terrarium. See pages 142-143 for instructions on planting a terrarium garden.

BOWL

SPHAGNUM

When new growth, still attached to mother leaf, is about this size, it's ready to shift from original pot into regular potting soil.

When new plants are 2 or 3 inches tall, they may again be shifted to the next larger size pot. You can separate each rosette and plant individually, or pot the entire clump together.

When potting plants, put a piece of broken clay pot or a bottle cap over bottom hole to insure drainage without washing away soil. Hold plant in center of pot, fill around it.

Geraniums—old-fashioned
favorites that are now back in vogue!

Great-grandmother prized them, and so will you! Never really forgotten, the geranium was neglected for a good many years. But it's had big new popularity recently, with scores of lovelier varieties being regularly developed as a result.

It's easy to see why geraniums are such popular plants. Their big heads of bloom look like gay, little umbrellas; their foliage has a spicy scent; and they're always cheerful about growing indoors in winter as house plants, then moving outdoors for the summer to brighten porch, terrace, garden.

Geraniums like lots of sunshine

Rather undemanding plants in most matters, geraniums won't tolerate shade. Unless they get some sun each day, they grow "leggy," and refuse to bloom. To be successful with geraniums indoors, you should give them a spot in your sunniest window.

Temperatures ranging from 60° to 70° are ideal, and plenty of fresh air and high humidity help insure good performance.

Don't overwater potted geraniums

Potted geraniums do best when allowed to become quite dry between waterings. They are not one of the plants—like ferns—which are happy with roots constantly damp.

When you water, do it thoroughly—until water runs out of the bottom drainage hole. Then empty the saucer, and don't give water again until soil is quite dry to the touch.

Geraniums benefit from regular doses of plant food when in bloom, but fertilizing while they're in their dormant phase only makes plants grow overtall, spindly.

There's no prettier sight than →
a windowful of geraniums

Geraniums, or *Pelargoniums*, to use their botanical name, come in hundreds of varieties. Colors range from commoner reds to white, pink, lavender.

Most widely grown are the zonal varieties, usually doubles, although there are attractive singles, too, with solid green or variegated leaves.

This amiable plant moves
outdoors in the summertime

Where space is small, a single geranium in an ample pot can do this and keep it up, week after week, through a summer. If you need larger outdoor color splashes, use 3 to 5 in 4-inch pots; sink them in the soil of a tub or plant box.

Exchange old for new plants by making cuttings twice each year

Geranium plants need regular pruning to keep them growing in bushy, pleasing shape. The stems you cut back can then be rooted to give you healthy, new plants.

Early in spring, get ready to plant your outdoor flower bed with cuttings taken from vigorous plant that's been growing indoors.

After rooting the cuttings—follow step-by-step directions on the opposite page—pot them up, and set them in a sunny window. They'll be ready for planting outdoors in from four to six weeks.

Then, in late summer, before there's any danger of frost, take cuttings from plants that have been blooming outdoors so you can again have blooms in the house, when your garden's gone to sleep for the winter.

Keep your plants full and bushy by a regular program of pinching back tips

This pink geranium is shapely and full of bloom because terminal growth was pinched back several times to get low, well-branched plant. As soon as flowering stems appear, pinching should be stopped, allowing the plant to go ahead and bloom. Water amply while plant is in bloom.

Follow these steps to start geraniums from cuttings

1 Take cuttings 3 to 5 inches long, cutting or breaking between joints, or just below where leaf's attached to main stem. Avoid both soft, immature and old, woody branches.

2 Trim lower leaves from cutting to allow for planting depth of about 2 inches. Be gentle in cutting or breaking off leaves and cut off no more than are absolutely necessary.

3 You can get cuttings to root faster in many cases by treating them with root stimulants or hormone powders. Dip cuttings into powder following instructions on package.

4 Set cuttings in vermiculite, perlite, or coarse sand. Keep moist—not soaking wet. Keep cuttings in light, not sunny location until roots begin to form; then move into sun.

5 Cuttings are ready to pot when roots are 1½ to 2 inches long—usually in 4 to 6 weeks. Set in 4-inch pot, providing for bottom drainage. Leave room to water at the top.

6 Pinching encourages branching on a young plant. When it's about 6 inches tall, use sharp knife or fingertips to pinch off the tip. Failure to do this makes stalk grow over-tall.

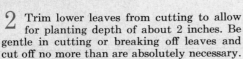

Flowering begonias bloom

Everblooming begonias are among the best of house plants, for they're so easy to grow, so faithful about putting forth their small blooms of pearly white, pink, or red.

The varieties pictured here are bedding begonias, inexpensive to buy in the spring and set outdoors for the summer. They go on flowering when you bring them indoors.

But because both plants and blooms are small, they won't look at all spectacular unless you grow and show them in quantity, as in the tree arrangement pictured across the page, or with many plants to a pot.

Grow as many as you want by making stem cuttings from the plants you have by the process pictured and described below.

Here's the easy way to multiply your everblooming begonias

Use sharp knife to make 4-inch cuttings from a mature plant. Make the cut on a slant. Remove enough of lower leaves to allow for inserting from 1 to 2 inches in rooting medium.

Fill shallow wooden or metal box with coarse sand, perlite, or vermiculite. Use pencil point to poke holes; insert cuttings to depth of 1 or 2 inches. Space plants so leaves don't touch.

When cuttings have developed roots that are about 1 inch long, it's time to move them to small pots. Supply bottom drainage; fill with regular potting soil; firm about roots; water.

In a few weeks, plant roots should fill soil ball in small pot. Check by tapping pot edge against table to remove plant. If roots have filled the ball, shift to permanent pot.

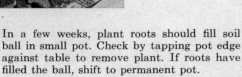

willingly, both indoors and outdoors

*They'll bloom constantly
in sun or in partial shade*

This is the variety of everblooming begonia called "Christmas Cheer Red." It's a bedding or edging type, also described as fibrous-rooted. The botanical name is *Begonia semperflorens*.

Its dusky, plum-colored foliage is a pleasant change from the green leaves of those which bear the pink or white flowers, like the plant pictured below. Cuttings are made in the same manner for all of them.

*Young plants you've grown from cuttings
of your bedding begonias will take on
fresh glamor when displayed in a wall tree*

WATERPROOF
CONTAINER

There's a secret to the success of this begonia "tree." It's the watertight cups in which the pots of begonias stand.

These cups make it practical to water the begonia plants as frequently as necessary with no fear of streaking the wall or of water spotting the floor.

Large ceramic container at the base is separate from the tree, and is planted with a large number of the young plants to give a full, bushy look at the base.

Tuberous begonias
for spectacular flowers in summertime

Tuberous begonias do best in partial shade, which makes them good choices for pots and window boxes where color is wanted.

Flower sizes run from 2 to as much as 8 inches in some of the singles. In shape, they resemble rosebuds, carnations, or the smooth semidouble and double camellias. And some are like giant crapemyrtle blossoms. Blooms are solid color except for those of the Picotee type which have deeper color in the margins of the flowers.

Partial shade, a loose, rich soil, protection from the wind, and moisture in the air and soil are the four requirements for the best success with begonias.

When the blooming period ends, tubers may be dried out, stored in plastic bags, and saved until the following year when they may be planted again for more blooms.

← *Venetian blind controls sunlight*

A south window equipped with a venetian blind makes it easy to regulate the amount of sunshine that reaches your tuberous begonias.

When you grow them in pots, you can move the plants that are loaded with blooms to the porch, terrace, or living-room table top, have color where you want it on short notice. Where you show them off is up to you.

Dress up the porch with begonias

Quick color in shade is yours if you suspend tuberous begonias of the hanging type like this from a tree limb or outer edge of porch roof. Make sure they don't get full sun through the middle of the day, and that they are protected from strong wind.

In the North, start tubers in pots in mid-March or mid-April for big summer blooms

Healthy, small tubers will flower, but larger ones send up more stems. For most spectacular show, select tubers at least 1½ inches across. Blooms of bush-type are larger than hanging-basket type.

To start tubers, use 6- to 7-inch pots. Fill each to 1 inch of rim. Press rounded side of tuber into soil as far as shoulder. Do not cover dished-in top until new sprouts are close to 3 inches tall.

Gloxinias put on a gorgeous show of

Success with gloxinias depends more upon proper watering than any other single factor. Test by squeezing some of the soil into a ball in the hand; if it falls apart when touched, water is needed.

Gloxinias also require a warm, moist atmosphere during growth and blooming. Put them in bright light, not in direct sun as it will cause sunscalding of foliage.

*A gloxinia's needs are much
like those of the African-violet* →

Open, porous soil, strong light but not burning sun, careful watering with tepid water — all these requirements of gloxinias are very close to those of African-violets.

It's also possible to reproduce them in the same fashion — by rooting leaves.

Easiest, quickest way to get showy gloxinia flowers is to start with healthy tubers

1 Depending on source, tubers can be bought from December through March. Tuber should show dry bits of last year's growth, maybe pinkish new growth on top side, roots below.

3 When new growth looks like this, lift the tuber and shift to regular potting soil. Use at least a 5-inch pot to allow for growth of roots; handle new roots quickly and gently.

2 Avoid rot by starting tuber in vermiculite, perlite, or coarse sand. Leave the fresh tip exposed. Add water at outer edge of pot; don't pour into the crown of the tuber.

4 Fill lower half of pot with potting soil. Hold tuber in one hand while sifting soil about it with the other. Tuber should sit high at finish. Firm soil down and water.

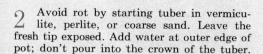

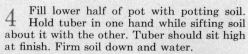

color that lasts for weeks as buds unfold

Amaryllis and its relatives for colorful show

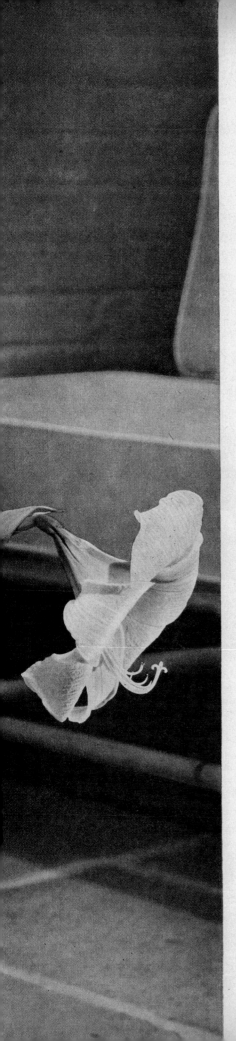

←

*Big modern bulbs are
treated to flower
in time for Christmas*

You can buy amaryllis bulbs
that have been "cold-treated"
by a secret process in Holland
for flowering on schedule during the holiday season.

Watching the flower stalks
shoot up and the fat buds ex-
pand and open will keep your
whole family in suspense.

For step-by-step directions
on planting the bulb, caring
for it during blooming and until next year's blooms are due,
see the following pages.

→

*Sprekelia grows in pot
or flower border*

Grow this unusual bulb as a
pot plant, like amaryllis, or
outdoors, like glads.

This one put forth its velvety scarlet flower just 8 days
after it was planted in a pot.

To grow outdoors, choose a
spot at front of flower border
so the short-stemmed flowers
show. Dig in fall; store over
winter, just as you would glads.

→

*Clivia bears orange
blossoms in midwinter*

Bulb-like but not a true bulb,
clivia, or Kafirlily, blooms
once a year, but its foliage
stays green all year through.

Plant and care for it just
as for an amaryllis except to
omit the drying-off period.

See page 2 for a color picture that shows you how handsome is this plant in bloom.

← *As exciting as fireworks is an amaryllis when it bursts into bloom*

Blooms come along rapidly after you plant an amaryllis bulb—some within 21 days. Their big trumpets of color are especially rewarding in a season when showy flowers are few. Choose from several shades of red, orange, salmon, or solid colors striped with white.

Four simple but important steps to follow when you first plant an amaryllis bulb

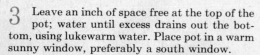

1   Size is important; bulb at right is too small; buy those which are 2½ inches in diameter or larger. Bulb should have some roots attached; *may* show new growth at top.

2   Supply bottom drainage. Use pot (6-inch or larger) big enough to leave an inch of space free around bulb. Place bulb so half of it is above soil level. Preserve all roots.

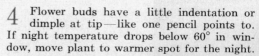

3   Leave an inch of space free at the top of the pot; water until excess drains out the bottom, using lukewarm water. Place pot in a warm sunny window, preferably a south window.

4   Flower buds have a little indentation or dimple at tip—like one pencil points to. If night temperature drops below 60° in window, move plant to warmer spot for the night.

for you year after year

*Your care after the flowers fade
decides the fate of next year's blooms*

Bulb uses up food reserves in producing flowers, then regains its strength through leaves and roots to make next year's bloom. You can help the process with plant food. Use dry or liquid form. Follow package directions.

As soon as blooms wither, cut off with razor blade or sharp knife, flush with stalk, so no stub remains. This prevents possible formation of seeds which would only rob bulb of strength. Continue watering; keep plant in the sun.

When frost danger passes, choose sunny outdoor location for the plant. Dig a hole that's deep enough so pot rim will be level with the surface of the soil, first placing some gravel at bottom of hole to guarantee good drainage.

Stalks begin to turn yellow shortly after the last flower fades. When this happens, they can be removed without causing the plant to "bleed." Cut stalk off where it emerges from the bulb, being careful not to injure leaves or bulb.

Water, feed through summer. Lift before first killing frost; store dry in basement for 2-3 months. Again bring to light; water. Now, as bulb hasn't been cold treated, it will revert to normal time of blooming—late in winter.

How to have an indoor spring many weeks ahead of time

← *Play a gentle deception on spring flowering bulbs*

By a process known as "forcing" (meaning to bring to bloom at earlier than normal date) these daffodils and crocus were coaxed into flowering indoors far ahead of those outdoors. The following pages tell you how to do it.

Hyacinths, daffodils, and → tulips are the easiest

The larger the bulb, the simpler it is to force. And you can advance your chances of success by asking for early varieties of these bulbs. The later the bulb blooms outdoors, the harder it will be to force indoors successfully.

1 To succeed in forcing, it's important to plant healthy bulbs firmly in good soil. Give enough water to dampen the soil.

2 In warm areas, delay planting till cold weather. Soil temperatures should be below 48°, but bulbs shouldn't freeze.

3 Allow at least 12 weeks of cold weather to pass before you lift pots and bring indoors to 60° basement temperatures.

4 Make sure roots fill pot, tops are several inches tall before bringing pots indoors. Unpot and check roots to be certain.

Wake bulbs early from a winter sleep

Sink spring bulbs outdoors for three months of cold weather; bring indoors to bloom

1 Set bulbs in pots so noses are just below the pot rim. Don't overcrowd. Firm soil down with your fingers. Water.

2 Set pots in trenches with rims 1-2 inches below soil level. Stakes and labels help to locate and identify pots later.

3 When shoots are 1-3 inches tall, bring the pots indoors. Keep dark, at 60° for a week; then move to a sunny window.

For looks and fragrance →
hyacinths are one of
choicest bulbs to force

There are hyacinth bulbs on the market which flower indoors if grown in water. But there is a greater danger of bulb rot with this method of forcing than if bulbs are sunk in soil outdoors, and brought indoors to flower.

Flowers last longer if plant is removed from full sun before flower heads are fully opened.

←

Golden daffodils and
deep, purple crocus
offer good color contrast

You can depend on King Alfred daffodils to force easily. Put several in a pot for show.

Crocus isn't quite so certain to force satisfactorily. It's best to bring pot into light as soon as you lift it from trench. But keep it cool for a week before putting it in a sunny window, just as with bigger bulbs.

From the time you plant spring flowering bulbs in your garden until they bloom, a period of 7 to 8 months elapses. By forcing, you can cut that time in half.

To succeed, you should duplicate—but shorten—the stages bulbs blooming in the garden pass through. They are: (1) fall planting (in pots sunk outdoors); (2) prolonged cold weather (this period is reduced to about 12 weeks in forcing); (3) warmth and sunshine to bring buds to flower.

When planting, supply bottom drainage; use bulb pans (shallower than the standard pots) if available. Plant bulbs as shown in the sketch on the opposite page.

Select a site for your outdoor trench where sun reaches it, softens soil, makes it easy for you to lift pots when proper time arrives. A south location is best for this reason.

It will also be easier to lift pots without breakage if you line trench with dry leaves or excelsior before setting pots into it. Then cover with another protective layer before filling trench with soil.

Don't sink pots too deep. Rims shouldn't be more than a couple of inches below level of soil. Mound up raked leaves over top of trench for extra protection; keep leaves from blowing off by laying a board on top.

After at least 12 weeks of cold weather have elapsed, lift a pot and check to see if roots have formed, and shoots are up before bringing bulbs indoors to force.

Move pots first to basement (or location where temperature isn't above 60°) for a week. Keep watered and away from light during this period. Then bring to sunny window and watch buds swell, flowers open.

A longer life for your gift plants

Delight over a blooming plant can turn to keen disappointment if you don't know how to give it proper care. And you can feel quite resentful—unjustifiably so—if you mistakenly assume that all plants should live on indefinitely, as do many foliage plants.

Some of the seasonal flowering plants must be looked upon is if they were cut flowers—to be enjoyed while they last, and to be discarded when they fade.

A number of those we traditionally give and receive cannot live long except under greenhouse conditions—so different from the desert-like atmosphere that characterizes most of our homes in winter.

With few exceptions, seasonal blooming plants will last longest in your home if you give them a cool, bright location and plenty of water of a room temperature. It takes lots of water to produce blooms, and water requirements should be checked on faithfully each day so the plant will never wilt.

You may like to toast your legs over a hot air register, but most plants give up and die a rapid death in such a location. Blasts of cold air are equally unwelcome, so choose a spot that's away from drafts.

Don't let all these cautions prevent you from using flowering plants as decorations in spots that are unsuitable as long-time homes. Just remember to move the plant back to a more congenial location when it has served its temporary purpose as a handsome centerpiece or end table decoration.

You'll like its distinctive blooms and marbled leaves

A fine, big cyclamen plant you buy from your florist may have only five or six blooms showing. But look down into the heart of the plant and you will see dozens of tiny buds.

They'll all push their way up and bloom if you give the plant a sunny window and lots of water. In this, it is an exception to the general rule that seasonal, blooming plants last longer out of sun. Pour water in at pot edge, not into plant crown.

Poinsettias come in pink, white plus Christmas red →

This plant is easily damaged by chilling. Keep in warm, draft-free spot.

After colorful bracts have fallen off, you may want to experiment with holding it over for another season of bloom. If so, shift to a cool location (near a basement window, perhaps), water only occasionally.

When warm weather comes, cut stems back to no more than 8 inches; set it out in garden, in sunny location. Bring indoors well before frost.

Keep your gift plants away from blasts of

Check daily to see that the plants are getting enough water

← *Jerusalem-Cherry plant has bright orange fruit that resembles the cherry tomato*

This plant is related to the garden tomato and, like it, wants plenty of sun, ample moisture. Give it what it needs, and it will stay fresh and attractive for several months or more.

If you'd like to grow your own plant next season, save some of the "cherries" as they drop off; dry them.

Early in spring, plant seeds in pots indoors. When frost danger has passed, sink pot in sunny garden spot. Bring it indoors before cold weather; have a new Jerusalem-Cherry plant!

Ornamental pepper plants can be reproduced in the same fashion.

A bloom-laden azalea will → keep its show for many weeks

Keep your azalea plant in good light but in a fairly cool location if you want it to last as long as possible. It will probably need to be watered each day. Check daily to make sure.

Once it stops blooming, resign yourself to discarding it—unless you live in an area where winters are mild. In that case, set it outdoors in spring, handling as any sun-loving shrub.

← *Christmas begonia gives you lavish amounts of bloom*

Given plenty of water, the Christmas begonia will stay covered with bloom for weeks. But enjoy the gorgeous color while you can. When it's through, it's through and must be discarded.

The lush growth comes from energy stored in the plant, grown under hothouse conditions. When that has been exhausted, the plant is generally too weak to repeat the flowery show.

hot or cold air and make them last longer

Chapter 4

Potted plants that move outdoors

A summer out of doors is of real benefit to most house plants. Nearly all like the brighter light they can get on porch, patio, or in the garden. But not all like direct sun, as do the geraniums and coleus pictured here. Others need protection also from strong winds and beating rains.

Follow the advice on the following pages in choosing the outdoor location which is best for your favorite house plants.

Big pots of blooming geraniums →
convert any spot to a flower garden

In a tiny back yard, most of its surface covered with concrete, a few pots of bright geraniums produce a colorful accent.

Geraniums won't flower this freely unless they get lots of sunshine. And you should pinch back ends before blooms come on to get a bushy and shapely plant.

If you want to have prize coleus plants, give them a summer in the garden

Because they're such sun-lovers, coleus plants grown indoors are apt to get "leggy" in a hurry. But if you break off tops, they root easily in sand or water.

Take stem cuttings early in spring from house plants; have them ready to set outdoors as soon as warm weather arrives. Sink pots as shown, or set the plants directly into the ground.

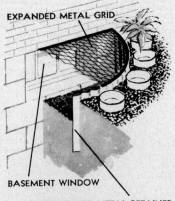

EXPANDED METAL GRID

BASEMENT WINDOW

CORRUGATED METAL RETAINER

In a tub or in

Bring color to a partly shaded spot

Rose-rainbow coleus plants and everblooming begonias make brilliant companions for edging plants like exacum used here in a partly shaded location. Take cuttings at end of summer to carry indoors.

Geraniums in pots for patches of color

Fill in bare spots or gaps in a flower border with portable color—geraniums in pots. Striking containers do much to enhance the simplest of plants, make them suitable in sophisticated surroundings.

*Garden in pots adds
style to deck-type terrace*

Philodendron plants move outdoors and get partial shade in a shadow-box arrangement.

Japanese maples are impressive in square, wooden tubs. Totem-pole plantings or big specimens of many foliage plants are possible substitutes if there is protection against too-hot sun.

Potted mums are massed for color impact, easy tending. ↓

a border, potted plants give quick color

Want to dress up a porch or patio, inject extra color in your flower border? Look to potted plants for an easy solution.

There are two ways to do it. The simplest is to buy sturdy, young plants from florist or greenhouse in spring. Group several in a large pot or in the garden for a good showing through the summer months.

If you have the indoor space to handle it, preferably a large, sunny basement window shelf, you'll also enjoy the other way—making your own cuttings indoors in early spring. When warm weather arrives, you're ready with a crop of young plants.

Of the popular house plants, several are extremely easy to propagate by cuttings. Geraniums, coleus, everblooming begonias are among the most obliging. Chrysanthemums can be rooted this way, too, but success is less certain than with those just named.

Change the scene when you like with gardens you grow in pots!

Fancyleaf caladiums give you summer-long outdoor color

Choose leaves of crimson, rose, pink, or white mottled with green. A 7-inch pot will hold about 3 tubers. Start indoors in early spring for summer show. Don't cover tubers more than an inch deep. Grow in partial shade.

Give tuberous begonias the prominent display they deserve →

Out-of-this-world quality of tuberous begonias shows off to wonderful advantage when pots are hung on a garden fence. Begonias should receive direct sun only in the mornings.

After you move plants outdoors, use a fine spray when you water them; remember they need frequent watering.

Move in with potted plants if you want to rush the season

Once the spring bulb show is over, the average garden looks a bit bare until summer blooms come along. Fill in the gap with potted plants like these to brighten a garden wall. Have color in the place and at the time you want it.

←

*Dappled sunlight is perfect
for many of your foliage plants*

A back-yard fence like this one which is
equipped with staggered shelves to accommodate potted plants has many virtues.

It gives protection from wind and too-
strong sunlight; it makes the most of a
small amount of space; it masses plants so
they take on importance.

Almost all of the ferns, vines, and common foliage plants you grow indoors in
winter would find such a setting as this
ideal for the summer months.

They'll love a summer holiday!

The outdoor life is as appealing to most
house plants as it is to people during the summer months. When *you* move out to patio or
back yard, take your house plants along.

Indoors, it's almost impossible to give them
all the light and humidity they need for a long
and healthy life. But if they can spend their
summers outdoors, they will store up enough
energy to last a long time under less-than-
perfect indoor conditions.

Use discretion in choosing a location. Give
tender foliage plants a summer home on a
shaded porch or in a wall niche like the one
pictured at the top of the page. Others, like
geraniums, succulents, cactus, will revel in
the sunniest spot you can find.

Make a plant box to match a back-yard fence

Both plant box and back-yard fence are of grape stakes. Into
the box is set a row of house plants, still in their clay pots. Because it's a sunny location, graceful ivy and bright geraniums
were wise selections. If you want to copy the idea for a shadier
location, try caladiums and grape-ivy instead.

How to have a garden at doorstep

Rustic garden bench is twice as inviting as an
outdoor sitting area because of the plants
grouped around it. And it takes only a few to
give a true garden atmosphere to a paved,
outdoor area such as this.

The same sort of treatment—wall brackets
for vining plants, tubs for upright ones—
would work equally well on a screened porch.

←

Set a row of potted plants
to bloom along garden path

Here's an idea to appeal to any city dweller with limited garden space and a liking for plants.

Set a row of pots along a garden path—with a fence serving as background and windbreak—to get the equal in looks of a much bigger area planted the usual way.

Caution: remember that plants in pots dry out quicker than the ones growing in the ground.

Cactus and succulents
like a season in the sun

Shallow metal saucers—a Japanese borrowing—make good showcases in which to display outdoors a collection of cactus and succulents.

Their root systems are so shallow that no damage will result if you unpot them and plant them in the proper soil mixture for the summer; repot to bring indoors in the winter months.

Give big plants protection

Summer winds can blow strong. So if you plan to set one of your big plants outdoors, be sure you give it a safe location.

Next-to-the-fence placement is wise. And a heavy tub for a container is further guarantee against its being toppled and broken.

Succulents that flourish where it's

hot and dry

Massed succulents make a show of color

Sedums in bloom are set in the foreground, kalanchoes at center, and 3-foot-tall cotyledons at back of this planting.

The big danger in setting succulents into the ground is rot. If you live in a climate where summer rains are heavy and frequent, better not risk it.

Instead, set your succulents outdoors in pots, where drainage is controllable and good.

Variety is endless and care the simplest

Small, beadlike-leaved sedums come in a bewildering array of varieties. They are eye-arresting for color and formation.

Echeverias in rosette shapes put up graceful flowering stems during the summer months.

Unless it rains very seldom, you probably will not need to water them at all. Be sure the pots they grow in have adequate bottom drainage, and give them a bright and sunny location.

Succulents show off best in family huddles

Single plants in the succulent family may be unimpressive. In a grouping—easy to achieve if plants are in pots—you can secure striking effects.

Echeverias, sedums, agaves, and aloes are some of the heat-loving succulents shown here.

Be sure to bring succulents indoors well in advance of winter weather. One light frost could wipe them out!

Planters
put color where you want it, indoors or out

The plants you set outdoors for the summer will look handsomer, be simpler to shift if they're grouped in a plant box.

Indoors, too, it is often advantageous to move plants about—from the place where they show off best to the place where they can get needed sun between showings.

Inexpensive to build, a planter similar to those pictured here requires no expert carpentry, can be put together by anyone who's handy with hammer and saw.

Casters are almost a must if the plant box is primarily for indoor use. For an outdoor planter not equipped with casters, try one of our moving tips sketched opposite.

Metal strips trim a simple redwood box

Planter of simplest construction is rectangular in shape. Its polished metal corners give it an indoor look. The casters with which it is equipped make moves easy, even when it's loaded with heavy pots.

When you build your own plant boxes, you can modify the dimensions to suit your wants

1 In a standard-width lumber, this box uses 1x12s, is 30 inches long. Have yours any wanted length. Beveled 2x8 base is recessed to take the casters.

2 Coat metal, hand grips, end-grain at once with plastic sealer as a protection against tarnishing, discoloration. Waterproof inside of planter.

3 Black plant tub was a mackerel pail. Soaking, paint, brass strips, knobs have transformed its looks.

Rustic style suits this planter to outdoor living

Scored wood paneling is used for the body of this box, with plain wood trim. It is being moved into place by rolling along paved surface of terrace on three sections of pipe to avoid heavy lifting.

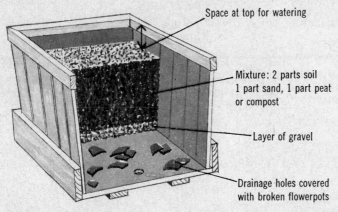

Space at top for watering

Mixture: 2 parts soil 1 part sand, 1 part peat or compost

Layer of gravel

Drainage holes covered with broken flowerpots

Success with plants grown in plant boxes depends on good drainage, right soil mixture, care in giving proper amount of water.

Old pair of roller skates supplies mobility. Saw off heel flanges; remove front clamps. Bore holes in the platform of each skate and bolt to cleat underneath.

Paint the inside with an asphalt emulsion or with a waterproof paint to protect wood from moisture.

Five ways to avoid strain when you move planters

Use your snow shovel as a skid. Best on grass, smooth surfaces.

Heavy burlap, canvas make good slings for a move across paving.

Borrow Junior's wagon for long hauls. Planks add extra width.

"Egyptian carry" works if you have a helper. Use rope, 2x4s.

For short distance move, use pipe lengths; rotate from front to back.

Detailing adds refinement to basic planter

An almost-rustic planter looks graceful because of trim and careful attention to details. Diagonal kerfs and concave accents identify it as a real job of craftsmanship. Directions below show you how you can build one like it.

Sturdy designs

For one important planting to decorate a terrace or patio, use a planter big enough to be noticed, sturdy enough to be suitable in its outdoor setting. Any of the four pictured here will fill the bill.

Whatever style of outdoor planter you decide to build, follow these general rules to insure good looks and healthy plants:

(1) Miter all outside corners for a neat look and a tight fit.

(2) Raise box so air can circulate under it, protect against mildew and rot.

(3) Sink all nailheads; fill with putty.

(4) Sand all corners and edges smooth.

(5) Paint inside of box with an asphalt emulsion or some other wood preservative.

(6) Bore holes in bottom and spread a 1-inch layer of broken pottery or gravel on bottom before you set plants in place. This will guarantee good drainage.

Basic construction is simple and detailing can be added with a power saw and drill

You'll need 5/4-inch stock, 12 inches wide; 1-inch stock is too thin. Taper sides to 11-inch base, and miter to fit. Or, use butt joints and metal angles to brace the joints.

Sketch at right shows how scrap lumber and dowel provide steady pivot point while concave cut is being made. You need four dowels, 2½ inches long, one for each side.

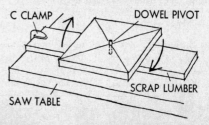

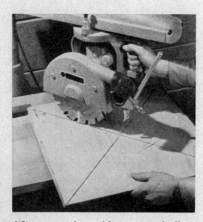

After tapering sides, cut shallow kerfs on the diagonals as shown. Or do this with a small chisel if you prefer to have wider kerfs than these.

Drill pilot hole for dowel where saw cuts across. Then, in piece of scrap wood, drill another hole to accept dowel which is serving as pivot.

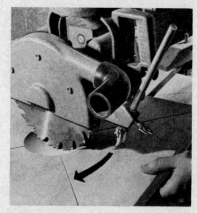

With pivoting jig in place, rotate sides on dowels; turn down setting on saw as you cut. Remove dowel, coat with glue; reinsert as plug.

for an outdoor box

Sturdy frame gives grip for fingertips

For plants with big root systems, here's a planter large enough to accommodate them. Top facing adds a finished look and supplies a convenient surface on which to set pots or tools while working.

Before planting, coat the inside of the box with waterproofing material. To take care of drainage, start with a 1-inch layer of gravel; add another inch of gravel for each 6 inches of soil it takes to fill the box from this point to the top. Fill rest of space with equal parts of gravel, garden loam and peat moss for a healthy soil mixture.

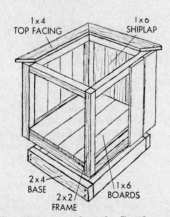

Saw twelve 2x2s same length. Set four upright as pillars. Nail the rest in between, top and bottom, to form rigid frame. Nail on bottom planks, cover with shiplap or siding, as you prefer. Set planter onto a recessed pedestal made with 2x4s.

For a new look, try a hexagonal box

For a six-sided box, start by drawing a pattern of a perfect hexagon on paper — as in diagram shown at left. Transfer to wood and cut out the base.

Cut side pieces to fit base. Use cleats to fasten them on.

Outer strips trim an inner framework

To make this square plant box, use a miter box to saw the ends of the facing strips at a 45-degree angle. Assemble and attach to square base.

Space 1x2-inch strips ¾ inch apart; nail to inner framework.

Chapter 5

How to grow
healthy plants

Light, soil, water—these are the big three factors that determine the health of your house plants. Requirements for each of the three elements vary from plant to plant, but the variables are neither so great nor so mysterious as you may think if you're a beginner at indoor gardening.

Once you know that most of the foliage plants we call "house plants" are natives of tropical forests, you understand why they flourish in a subdued light—as if filtered down through leafy trees—rather than in full sun that scorches tender leaves.

For the same reason, these plants prefer moisture in the air (though many are extremely tolerant of the near-desert conditions that prevail in our homes in winter), and moist, porous soil resembling the forest loam their ancestors once took root in.

The drawing below charts the way a plant manufactures its food from the soil, water, light, air that are its environment.

In the pages to follow, you'll find basic information on light, soil, and water requirements of average house plants, plus specific data on special needs of favorites.

Choose the right plant

Consult the table on the facing page for help in selecting the plants that will grow best in the home conditions you can offer.

If you have no sunny window, better pass up geraniums. If you want a vine in a dimly lit spot, grow grape-ivy rather than English ivy. If you've had bad luck in past, pick a "cinch-to-grow" plant that can thrive in less-than-perfect growing conditions.

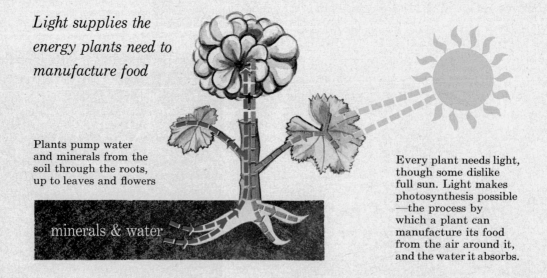

Light supplies the energy plants need to manufacture food

Plants pump water and minerals from the soil through the roots, up to leaves and flowers

minerals & water

Every plant needs light, though some dislike full sun. Light makes photosynthesis possible —the process by which a plant can manufacture its food from the air around it, and the water it absorbs.

FLOWERING PLANTS *for color and for seasonal accents*

PLANT	HEIGHT	LIGHT*	SPECIAL NOTES
African-violets	to 6 inches	medium	Use porous soil mixture. Keep cold water off leaves.
Amaryllis	20-30	high	Plant high in pot. Give sun and food after flowering.
Begonias	6-24	high	Grow fast, need repotting oftener than most house plants.
Spring flowering bulbs	6 up	high	Need 10 to 12 weeks of cold; keep dark until well sprouted.
Geraniums	6-18	high	Many varieties. Allow soil to dry out occasionally.

FOLIAGE PLANTS *for all-year-long effectiveness*

PLANT	HEIGHT	LIGHT	SPECIAL NOTES
Aluminum plant	8-15	medium	Pinch to keep thick. Spray with water in dry weather.
Bromeliads	2-10	medium	Have small root systems—will grow well in small pots.
Dieffenbachia	to 60	low or medium	Leaves tip-burn if humidity is low. Avoid drafty location.
Ferns	6-20	medium	Use a light soil mixture with lots of organic matter.
Monstera	tall	low or medium	Also called cutleaf philodendron. Moist atmosphere best.
Palms	6 up	medium	Grow well in low light if given a good moisture supply.
Peperomia	6-12	low or high	Many varieties. Need light, well-drained soil.
Rubber plant	tall	any exposure	Sensitive to overwatering. Air layer when it gets spindly.
Schefflera	tall	low or medium	Grows best when kept on the dry side in a warm room.

VINING PLANTS *for planters, moss sticks, or hanging baskets*

PLANT	HEIGHT	LIGHT	SPECIAL NOTES
English ivy	—	high	Likes humidity high, drainage good, occasional sun bath.
Episcias	—	medium	Semi-trailing. Give care similar to that for African-violets.
Grape-ivy	—	low	Tolerates low light situations very well.
Philodendron	—	low-medium	Many varieties. Extremely adaptable. Grows in water or soil.
Devil's ivy	—	medium	Sometimes mistakenly called variegated philodendron.
Nephthytis	—	medium	Grows upright while young; twines as it grows older.

CINCH-TO-GROW *plants, tolerant of most growing conditions*

PLANT	HEIGHT	LIGHT	SPECIAL NOTES
Aspidistra	tall	any	Called "cast-iron" plant for its hardiness. Grows slowly.
Coleus	6-12	medium-high	Many colors; brighter if in sun. Roots easily from cuttings.
Jadeplant	6-24	medium-high	Keep on the dry side. Old plant becomes treelike.
Screwpine	tall	medium-high	Thrive in sunny, dry, hot situations. Do not overwater.
Spider plant	—	any	Trailing plant; roots from offsets. Tolerates low light.
Sansevieria	6-20	any	Withstands adverse conditions of low humidity and light.

*For more detailed information on light requirements, see following pages.

Watering

Moisten all of the soil

When you water from the top, add enough so water drains out bottom to be sure you've moistened all the soil. Use a saucer to catch drainage, and protect the surface on which the plants are placed.

Wick-water from bottom

Special self-watering flowerpots have a built-in reservoir that feeds water to soil through a wick. Or you can devise one with fiberglass wick, disk to hold pot above water, a deep dish to hold water.

"How often shall I water my house plants?" is the question asked by all beginners at growing plants indoors. The correct answer, "That depends . . . " is not so satisfying as some rule-of-thumb reply like "once a week" might be. But it's the only accurate reply.

Your home in winter may be almost as arid as a desert, and your plants will need far more water then than during humid summer weather. Small pots dry out more rapidly than big ones, so must be watered more frequently. Plants in bloom need more water than at other times.

But, in general, variations in water needs from plant to plant aren't great. Except for cactus and succulents, which tolerate drouth, all plants grow best in moist soil.

Add water whenever top soil feels dry to the touch—whether this be daily or weekly. When you water, do a thorough job. Supply enough to moisten soil all the way to the bottom. Wait to water again until top soil is once more on the dry side.

Top versus bottom watering

The diagrams at left show you two satisfactory ways of watering. If you water from the top, be sure to have broken crockery, pebbles or other loose material at the bottom of the pot for good drainage.

If you water from the bottom, don't use drainage material. Instead, insert a wick (preferably of fiberglass) to absorb water from a dish below, keep soil uniformly moist. Or you may purchase self-watering pots in a variety of styles and sizes.

Whether you water from top or bottom, it's good practice to give plants an occasional "dunking." Place pot in a pail or dish of water so it is half submerged. Leave it there until the surface of the soil is moist. Set plant aside and drain off surplus water before returning it to its usual location.

Don't leave a pot standing in water more than an hour or so. Too much water over a long period prevents oxygen from getting to roots, and roots must have oxygen to live.

Feeding

A little plant food goes a long way—too much may burn the roots and actually kill a plant. The various brands of fertilizer on the market differ in their strength, so follow exactly the directions on the package.

Older plants benefit from a light feeding every two or three months, except during the winter, when it is best to feed somewhat less frequently. New plants obtained from your florist need no fertilizer for the first six weeks after you get them, or even longer.

Commercial fertilizers always tell on the package the proportions of nutrients they contain. Those usually present are nitrogen, phosphoric acid, and potash. When you see the figures 5-10-5 or 10-6-4, it is to the percentages of these elements, and in the order stated above, that reference is made.

When should you fertilize?

It's not wise to assume that any sickly looking plant will benefit from a dose of plant food. The plant is more apt to be ailing because of too much water, too little light, too dry an atmosphere, or poor quality of the potting soil in which it's growing.

If your plant *is* suffering from starvation, nitrogen is most likely to be what it lacks. Symptoms are a yellow color in new leaves, and lack of vigor in new growth.

However, symptoms of injury from gas fumes, too much water, too little light are similar, except that when one of these is the culprit, you usually find lower leaves turning yellow, while those higher up stay green.

Dry plant foods come in powdered, granular, and tablet form. Or you can buy plant food as a liquid. Experiment with various types to see which gives you the best results.

When you use dry food, be careful not to get it onto the plant, and to water it into the soil at once. Tablets may be inserted into the soil at the outer edge of the pot, and will gradually be absorbed in the course of successive waterings.

The main thing to remember about fertilizers is "Don't kill a plant with kindness"!

Measure food accurately

Water dry food into soil at once to prevent burning. Regular lawn food works fine; half a teaspoon to a 6-inch pot is right amount. Apply commercial food exactly as the package directions state.

Tips on liquid fertilizer

When you use liquid plant food in solution, be sure to measure the water just as accurately as you do food. Use enough solution to moisten all soil—until the excess drains out of the bottom of pot.

Light

Houses are built for people—not plants. By a plant's standards, they're too dark, too dry, often too hot—like sunless deserts. The wonder is that so many plants survive.

Light needs of plants have received careful study by scientists in recent years, and the amateur indoor gardener now has at his command the results of their research.

The chart at the bottom of this page shows you how little light is actually available in places where house plants are grown. The tables on facing page group plants by minimum amounts of light needed if they are to prosper. Compare the two and you'll see that most plants just do not get enough light.

Effects of too little light

What happens when a plant gets too little light? Nothing, at first. Plants can survive for rather long periods on reserve food. But ultimately, new growth becomes spindly, new leaves smaller, and lower leaves die.

It may take only a few weeks, or as long as a year for a plant to show symptoms of light starvation. The cure is not a massive dose of light—which could kill a plant— but a return to adequate light conditions.

Nor is it wise to set foliage plants next to unshaded windows which face directly into the sun. Very few foliage plants can tolerate direct sunlight, especially when it is magnified by clear glass. Shifted to such a spot from a dim corner, they'll sunburn.

There are several ways you can give your plants more light: by moving them closer to windows, by moving them to brighter rooms, by leaving draperies and blinds open during the day. But the most convenient way is to supplement natural with artificial light.

You may use either incandescent lamps or fluorescent tubes to supplement sunlight. Spotlights, too, have been successful, and are decorative as well as functional.

For a more complete discussion of growing plants under artificial light, see the pages on that subject later in this chapter.

Determining light intensity

Charts and tables on these pages show you light measurements in terms of foot-candles. If you're a camera enthusiast, you're already familiar with this term which appears on light meters. Use yours, or borrow one, to make an accurate check on light in your home in places where you grow plants.

Lacking a light meter, you can calculate light intensity roughly if you know that at 500 foot-candles, you'll see a shadow outline cast by your fingers when your hand is placed between light source and plants.

Judge the light a plant gets from these typical readings

HOMES

General illumination	5 foot-candles*	
Reading or writing	20	"
Ironing and sewing	40	"
Workbench	40	"

HOTELS

Lobby	20 foot-candles	
Dining room	5 to 10	"

OFFICES

Typing, accounting	50 foot-candles

Conference room	30 foot-candles

STORES

Circulation areas	20 foot-candles	
Merchandising areas	50	"
Displays	100 to 200	"

OUTDOORS

Bright summer day	About 10000 foot-candles
Cloudy winter day	500 to 2000 "

*Amount of illumination at all points one foot from a uniform point source of one international candle.

Plants listed by minimum light needs for 16 hours a day

← *Need 15 to 25 foot-candles minimum*

LOW LIGHT

Aspidistra
Chinese Evergreen
Dieffenbachia amoena
Dieffenbachia picta
Nephthytis
Philodendron cordatum
Philodendron panduriforme
Philodendron pertusum
Sansevieria species
Schefflera

Need 25 to 50 foot-candles minimum →

MEDIUM LIGHT

Boston fern
Bromeliad species
Cissus rhombifolia
Dieffenbachia Rudolph Roehrs
Holly fern
Peperomia
Philodendron dubia
Devil's ivy

← *Need 50 to 100 foot-candles minimum*

HIGH LIGHT

Crotons
English Ivy
Ficus elastica decora
Ficus elastica doescheri
Ficus exotica
Ficus pandurata
Geraniums
Japanese fatsia
Kangaroo ivy
Mountain acanthus
Velvet plant

Note: These light intensities will keep plants alive for at least a year.

Potting and

1 Use ⅓ gravel for drainage; ⅓ peat to hold water, nutrients; garden or other soil makes up remaining third of a well-balanced potting soil mixture.

2 After putting in coarse material for drainage, fill soil in gently around tender roots; when pot is full, firm the soil down; leave room at top to water.

3 Water newly potted plant thoroughly; set in spot where it receives light, but not full sun until after it has become adjusted—two or three days.

Proper potting gives a plant the right start in life

Whether you begin with a seedling, a rooted cutting, a plant lifted from the garden, or a bulb, the way you first pot a plant is vital to its future health.

Most important of all is the quality of the potting soil in which your plant is to grow. With few exceptions, all house plants thrive in potting soil composed of gravel, peat, and soil in equal proportions—as illustrated in the top drawing at left.

You may make up your own potting soil mixture, or buy it commercially prepared. But whatever kind you use, be sure it is moist—not dry or wet. Tender roots "settle in" best, suffer least damage in moist soil. It's handy to keep some that's properly damp in a plastic bag, ready to use whenever it is needed.

Don't forget to put a layer of coarse material for drainage in the bottom of the pot before you begin to fill with potting soil. Broken chunks of clay pots or small rocks are satisfactory for this purpose. Omit this step if you are using one of the self-watering pots.

Consider looks, too, when you pot a plant. Your eye will tell you when a pot is of the correct size—in proportion to the plant.

Finally, if the plant is young and of a type which may be expected to grow rapidly, allow for this future growth in selecting the size of the pot. If you choose one too small, repotting will soon be necessary.

CLAY POTS come in sizes up to 14″. Standard size has a depth equal to top diameter; bulb, azalea pans are shallower.

CERAMIC OR PLASTIC pots without a drainage hole need a bottom layer of a coarse material to provide good drainage.

QUANTITY OF POTTING SOIL needed to fill standard 4″ flowerpot is 1 pint; for a 6″ pot, 3 pints; for an 8″ pot, 2 quarts.

repotting

Repotting older house plants stimulates healthy growth

A plant needs repotting when its roots get matted around the outside of the soil ball in which it is growing. Fast-growing plants should be checked every 3 or 4 months. Slow-growing plants may not need repotting more than once a year.

Ordinarily, it is best to shift a plant to a pot no more than an inch or two larger than its former pot. If the pot is too large in relation to the plant, the soil will dry out very slowly and it will be difficult for you to control the moisture—top soil may be very dry while central soil is still wet.

Normally, the roots of a pot-bound plant need not be disturbed at all when you set it into a larger pot, adding fresh potting soil at bottom, sides, and top.

But if the original soil ball has become packed down, had poor drainage, or too many soluble salts (from hard water), then all of the soil should be removed and replaced. Do this gently, so as to damage the roots as little as possible, and spread roots as you sift fresh potting soil around them.

Beginners are tense about damaging plants in the course of repotting, but it is really a simple operation to perform without injuring a plant. Water the day before repotting so that all of the soil ball will be slightly moistened. Then follow the three steps pictured at right to give your plant room for new and vigorous growth.

CLEAN POTS thoroughly before re-using. Steel wool makes quick work of removing encrustations from inside or outside of pot.

STERILIZE SOIL mixture if you believe it is infected. Bake moist soil mixture at 250° for 1½ hours in a closed container.

RULE OF THUMB dictates the amount of space—a thumb's width—you should leave free below pot rim to allow for water.

1 To remove plant, place fingers over soil ball; turn pot upside down. Tap on table edge. Plant will slide out. Matted roots mean repotting's due.

2 Cover hole in pot with bottle cap or bit of broken pot to keep soil from washing out. If pot's over 4″ deep, layer of gravel will improve drainage.

3 Set plant in new pot to test height. Add soil to bring to right height. Fill about roots with soil; press firmly with thumbs. Water, keep out of sun.

Adventures in greenhouse gardening

Once you become a truly dedicated indoor gardener, you'll covet a greenhouse of your own—whether it's a sizable private paradise like the one pictured across the page, or a miniature portable model like the one which is sketched below.

In winter months, there's nothing to equal the exhilaration of watching plants bloom in a greenhouse, while all outdoors remains bleak and frosty. And foliage plants, too, luxuriate in the warm, moist atmosphere a greenhouse can provide.

Types of greenhouses

Lean-to greenhouses (see sketch at right below) are in big demand because they can be attached to houses of almost all types and ages. They come in prefabricated form (as do also larger, freestanding ones) or they can be a "do-it-yourself" project.

Other types of attached greenhouses are the half-span and even-span, joined to the main building by metal flashings. The even-span greenhouse exposes more glass to the sunshine, is easier to erect.

In choosing a location for lean-to type of greenhouse, you'll find the southerly side of your house best—where it gets the most light. Morning sun is important; late afternoon sun counts for little.

Next to sunshine, heat and ventilation are most essential. You may be able to attach a greenhouse heating outlet to equipment you now have. Or you may want to invest in one of the compact, efficient heaters built for the purpose. Your local heating-equipment dealers can help you decide about this.

Don't build too small a house. It's difficult to ventilate and heat small areas under glass: temperature zooms when the sun comes up; drops almost as fast when it goes down or is blocked by clouds.

Ample ventilation by sashes in the roof and ends is also a necessity. A large opening or doorway into the house to which the greenhouse is attached is a great help—cuts down heat-absorbing wall space, provides an extra volume of air to cushion against rapid outside changes of temperature.

The most satisfactory way to ventilate is by means of a thermostatic control which automatically opens and shuts vents when the temperature rises above or falls below the wanted degree of heat.

One final need, where winters are severe, will be a good masonry foundation that goes well below the frostline, for protection.

Greenhouse preview of spring →

This lean-to greenhouse is part of a recent remodeling and joins a family room made from a two-car garage. Floor of greenhouse is sunk 18 inches, letting you look down on flowers.

Greenhouse gardening can be done on any scale—small or large

PORTABLE indoor types have glass or plastic tops, sides, let you grow orchids, root cuttings, raise plants from seed. This one includes fluorescent fixture to supplement sun. Set on stand or table.

LEAN-TO greenhouses in prefabricated models may be bought knocked down— all parts cut to exact size and shape you want. Attach to south side if you can.

Indoor gardening under artificial light

You can grow luxuriant house plants in any spot in your home with the aid of man-made sunshine—electric light. Corners so dark they'd discourage even a cast-iron plant can be turned into good settings for the light-loving varieties by using the right amount of artificial light.

Most plants get too little light during the winter months, not only because of the low light intensity, but also because of short day length. To remedy this, the perfect winter situation for a house plant would be in daylight by day, with a boost from artificial light during both daylight and dark hours.

But there are many plants which will live and thrive for varying periods of time on nothing but artificial light, in amounts the average indoor gardener can supply at a moderate cost. African-violets, begonias and gloxinias are some that will reach impressive proportions without ever catching a glimpse of the sun.

Where to locate a light setup

Enthusiasts for gardening under artificial light have placed their setups all over the house—from living room to basement, even in closets! But if you intend to grow a large number of plants, and experiment with propagation from seeds and cuttings, your basement will perhaps be the best location. It will offer ample space, and a lower temperature than the upstairs—probably from 55 to 65 degrees—which is better for most varieties of house plants.

Also, young plants not yet ready for exhibition are out of sight until they reach a stage where you want to bring them into the lived-in rooms of your home for display.

You can, of course, start on as small a scale as you wish—one plant under a table lamp. If you use an incandescent bulb, have at least a 75-watt bulb, placed no more than four feet from foliage, no closer than two feet. A fluorescent tube, because it burns cooler, can be placed closer to plants.

There are many possible variations that will work well and be decorative, too. Try an enclosed plant case, such as the one pictured across the page, or some of the other setups sketched and described on following pages. All can be built by a handyman at moderate cost and economically operated.

You can use either incandescent of fluorescent lights for this kind of gardening. Experiments show that a combination of both fluorescent and incandescent light is better than either used alone. It is beneficial to supplement with some incandescent light, particularly when a "daylight" type of fluorescent tube is to be used.

Research studies indicate that a plant will live and stay attractive for at least a year if it is lighted for 16 hours daily with the minimum light intensity it needs. The list at the bottom of the page groups plants according to their minimum light requirements in terms of foot-candles per day. For further listings and discussion, see the pages on light earlier in this chapter.

To reduce your work, you will want to install an inexpensive automatic timer which will turn lights on and off as needed, without your having to remember them.

Here are plants which you can grow under artificial light

700-1000 foot-candles minimum

Achimenes
Beloperone guttata (shrimp plant)
Clivia
Coleus
Croton
Fuchsia
Gloxinia
Impatiens
Jerusalem cherry
Kalanchoe
Sedum

300-700 foot-candles minimum

Episcia
Hoya (wax plant)
Pilea (artillery plant)
Maranta (prayer plant)
Saintpaulia (African-violet)

25-300 foot-candles minimum

Philodendron species
Sansevieria species
Syngonium podophyllum
Pothos (scindapsus)

Two 40-watt fluorescent tubes supply energy for growing plants in a planting box of simple wood construction, with lath drainboard at bottom. Short plants are blocked up to same height as tall ones.

Garden under artificial lights becomes a boxful of color when lid is raised

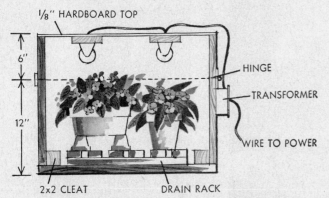

⅛" HARDBOARD TOP

6"

12"

HINGE

TRANSFORMER

WIRE TO POWER

2x2 CLEAT

DRAIN RACK

Cross-section view shows how plants are blocked up so all are same distance from light. Both cuttings and plants need 16 hours daily from two 40-watt tubes.

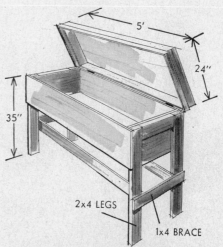

5'

24"

35"

2x4 LEGS

1x4 BRACE

Painting interior of box white increases light intensity. Hinged lid can be raised to control the humidity and temperature.

Light setups

*Basement plant box is easy
to build and maintain
in small amount of space*

If you use this unit for starting cuttings and seedlings, you can increase its efficiency by providing bottom heat. To do this, you can use a standard heating cable—such as is used in hotbeds. The cable should be thermostatically controlled, at an even temperature of about 75°.

With the unit closed, the uniform temperature will make control of the humidity easier. In an open unit, the effect of bottom heat on humidity would be difficult to evaluate.

Your local electrician will advise you concerning the installation of heating cable and thermostat.

*Grow flowering plants, root cuttings, seedlings with an
economical light-bench combination like this one*

Folding sawhorses, waterproof pans of 24-gauge galvanized metal, lights on pulleys, and a metal reflector create a winter garden. If using 85-watt fluorescent tubes, place 12 inches above plants; 60-watt incandescent bulb lights area 4x4 feet if suspended 2½ to 3 feet above plants. In either case, use light 16 hours a day.

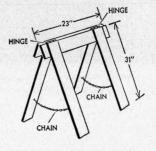

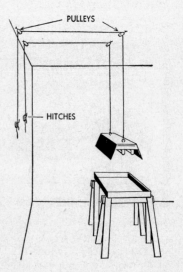

for your home

Here are four setups for growing plants under artificial light. Those across the page are for basement or seldom-used room, where looks are unimportant. Those on this page are attractive enough for lived-in portions of your home.

Any of these setups may be modified in dimensions to suit space you have. All will interest the indoor gardener who has more plants than window ledges, or few well-lighted spots.

If you want to grow seedlings and cuttings in quantity, you'll probably want to copy one of the constructions on the facing page, since they give you maximum space at minimum cost.

These two installations are equipped with bottom trays of waterproof metal you can line with sand or sphagnum moss. By keeping the bottom layer moist, you can reduce the frequency with which you'll need to water. Also, evaporation from bottom layer will increase humidity of air surrounding plants. The air of an average home is too dry for most house plants, and they will be healthier in this atmosphere.

To reduce your work in operating any of these setups, it will be worthwhile to install an automatic timer.

Lighted plants serve as a room accent

Here's a plant cabinet that is both functional and decorative. The sliding glass doors give it a humid, greenhouse-like atmosphere, keep plants dustfree.

Shelves are staggered (see the cross-section view at right) so all plants can benefit from the light tubes which are located in the top of the case.

Heat generating transformer for light tubes is outside the cabinet. Bottom vents keep moisture from fogging glass doors.

To reduce work of watering, use self-watering pots, or insert a wick in each pot which will soak up water from metal tray holding several of the plants.

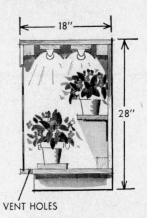

VENT HOLES

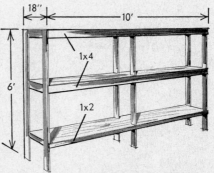

This wall-rack arrangement is suited to a family-room location where plants will get some daylight, with artificial light as a growing boost. Construction is simple, and measurements may be altered to suit the space you have.

Terrarium showcase for your plants

Like an oasis in a desert, a tiny, moist world of growing things inside a terrarium has an irresistible fascination. The glass garden invites you to paint your own scene, imitating nature on a miniature scale.

Dry, hot air of the house in wintertime is no handicap to plants in the terrarium, where moist air is trapped. Since moisture is so well conserved, a glass garden needs little water once it has been planted. An occasional sprinkling when surface soil feels dry to the touch is all that's necessary.

Preparing the container

Wash and polish the container so it will sparkle. Then place charcoal, gravel, and soil as shown in the diagram below. A lining of moss, green side out, between soil and glass is attractive.

A good soil mixture is 2 parts loam, 2 parts coarse sand, 1 part leaf mold—not so rich that your plants will rapidly outgrow their rather limited space.

Before you plant the terrarium, decide where you'll display it. If it's to be seen from one side, put larger plants in back, smaller ones forward. See the list below for plants that like a humid atmosphere.

Use the glass lid of your terrarium to control humidity and watering. If moisture condenses, remove the cover for a time. Place your glass garden in good light, but not in full sunlight, for this would trap too much heat and kill the plants.

Plants suitable for terrariums

Begonias (everblooming)
Baby's Tears
Fittonia
Ivy (miniature types)
Maranta
Palms (small)
Pteris (table ferns)
Peperomia
Saintpaulia (African-violet)
Woods plants: evergreen seedlings; dogtooth violet, Dutchman's breeches; hepatica; varieties of mosses; mushrooms.

Garden in glass keeps plants glossy and green in moist air

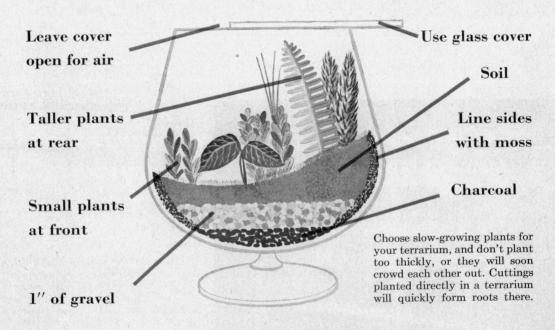

Leave cover open for air

Taller plants at rear

Small plants at front

1″ of gravel

Use glass cover

Soil

Line sides with moss

Charcoal

Choose slow-growing plants for your terrarium, and don't plant too thickly, or they will soon crowd each other out. Cuttings planted directly in a terrarium will quickly form roots there.

For an effective arrangement have a plant of major interest near the front and center of terrarium

Use your artist's eye when you choose plants and arrange them in your glass garden. Make miniature hills and valleys by mounding up or scooping away the earth.

Try to place each plant so it will present a pleasing contrast of shape and color with its neighbors — variegated foliage next to the solid, colorful next to green, and so on.

Remember that half the charm is the small-scale effect. As plants grow too large, replace with cuttings or plants of right size.

How to tell what ails a sick house plant

There's a remedy for the ailing plant, once you know the cause of trouble

1 LIGHT

If your plants are getting too little light, they may not show any ill effects for a short period of time. They will continue to produce new leaves by using stored energy.

If light is insufficient for a longer period, new stems become spindly. Foliage gradually becomes yellow-green. Eventually, all growth stops and plant dies.

To cure light starvation, move the ailing plant to a sunny window, or give it an extra amount of light artificially in the evening. For plants in stationary planters where you know light is consistently insufficient, it is wise to install an overhead light to supplement whatever daylight reaches them.

Plants in the home seldom get an overdose of light. If they've been accustomed to filtered light, rays of direct sun will burn them. Or, if you place them close to a window, the glass can intensify the heat enough to do severe damage to tender leaves. Too much sun produces burned spots on foliage.

Different plants require varying amounts of light. In general, the foliage plants can survive with considerably less light than those which produce flowers. Choose the right plant for the light situation you can offer and you'll have few light troubles.

2 PLANT FOOD

Plants manufacture their food from the air and the soil in which they grow by a process called photosynthesis, in which light is the source of energy. Fertilizers supply essential minerals, of which nitrogen is an important one and often unavailable in sufficient quantity for healthy growth. If there is too little food, the new leaves may be smaller than normal, and perhaps will be lighter in color. Growth will be slow, and both stems and leaves will be smaller than normal. To cure, adopt a regular feeding program for the undernourished plant.

You can use the same fertilizer that you put on your lawn. Or you can buy fertilizers especially made for house plants. They come in powder, liquid, or tablet form. Follow directions carefully.

If there is too much food, applied accidentally or carelessly, the roots of your plant may be burned. The plant will then wilt even when the soil is moist.

To cure this trouble, flush extra plant food out of the soil with lots of water. Or repot it in fresh potting soil.

Don't assume that every plant which looks sick is in need of a quick dose of fertilizer. Check to be sure trouble is not due to some other cause of poor plant health.

3 WATER

If a plant receives too little water, it will wilt. This seldom causes serious damage unless it occurs frequently, and then it stunts growth and causes flower drop.

Too much water is more common. The first symptom is usually the dropping of lower leaves. New leaves may continue to appear on top, but an overwatered plant gets leggy and bare of foliage at the base.

If you suspect that a plant has had too much water, tap it out of its pot and look at the roots. Root tips should be white. If they are brown, repot in loose, spongy soil mixture; and water less frequently.

Moisture in the air is also important to a number of house plants. It is difficult to supply in adequate amounts under average wintertime home conditions, where air is consistently warm and dry. If there is too little humidity over a period of time, the leaf tips of some plants will turn brown.

and give first aid

You can increase the amount of humidity in the immediate vicinity of the plants if you grow them in a metal plant box or tray lined with pebbles. Set pots onto this layer and keep moist. Evaporation will increase the humidity of the air layer just above and surrounding the plants.

If you use this method, you must not have water deeper than the pebbles, for drainage action through the bottom hole of the pot must continue to take place. If the pot stands in water, the roots will receive less oxygen and they will rot, just as when you overwater a plant from the top.

4 PESTS, DISEASES

Plants grown indoors will seldom be attacked by insects or disease if you buy them from a reputable florist.

The only disease—as distinct from infestation by insects—which occurs often enough to consider here is caused by soil-borne, rot-producing organisms. In young plants, it is known as "damping off." In older plants, it is called "stem rot." As there is no effective remedy, a plant that has this disease should be destroyed promptly.

What to do about insects

Those insects that attack house plants can be controlled with the same chemicals used to eliminate similar pests outdoors. An aerosol house-plant bomb is both effective and convenient to use indoors. Follow the directions on the package.

To prevent any pests from getting a start, clean plants regularly by syringing them in the sink, or by cleaning their foliage with a soft, damp cloth. The water you use should be lukewarm. Support each of the leaves by holding the palm of your hand under it as you wipe the top clean.

Even with good care, pests occasionally gain a foothold. If they do, isolate the infested plants until you've destroyed the insects, so healthy ones won't be attacked.

Frequent cleaning, regular examination, and prompt treatment eradicate insects

Give them warm bath in sudsy water

Supplement monthly washing or wiping of foliage with a twice-a-year thorough job in soapy water.

Redspiders and mealy bugs are controlled by this type of treatment, followed by an application of an insecticide over the plant.

For scale, scrub leaves gently with a soft brush and then apply insecticide.

Check regularly for signs of insects

When you examine a plant, turn the leaves over and look at their underside—where most insects are active in their work.

The group of mealy bugs shown on the plant at right can easily be eradicated by a thorough sponging, followed by spraying with a house-plant insecticide. Isolate plant from others.

Treat promptly to eliminate scale

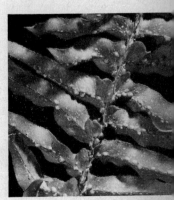

Protect plants from heavy scale infestation like this by inspecting them often.

Early treatment will prevent serious damage, is more effective than late attempts to cure the trouble.

To treat scale, purchase a spray designed specifically for that purpose.

Read label on insecticide bomb, follow instructions.

More tips on pest control, training,

Keep house plants greenhouse fresh with a regular program of care.

Good grooming for house plants is essential if you want them to serve as attractive ornaments for the rooms you live in.

Make it a practice to look at each plant with a discerning eye whenever you water it. If you see insects, suspicious looking spots or holes in foliage, begin treatment at once; isolate the plant promptly.

Does foliage look dusty? Carry with you a soft, damp cloth and wipe each leaf. Or take the plant to the sink and syringe it with a fine spray of lukewarm water.

Is the plant taking on a sprawling pattern of growth, or going to seed? Pinch back the ends of branches and remove yellowing or unattractive foliage to give a tidy, compact appearance, encourage new growth.

None of these jobs takes more than a few minutes. But if they're performed regularly, they'll make a world of difference in the appearance of favorite house plants.

A quick, convenient means of combatting almost any pest that attacks house plants is the handy "bomb" insect spray. No mixing required; and no cleanup afterward.

Follow the manufacturer's directions exactly for best results.

Cottony-white mealy bugs are a common house plant pest, with the African-violet as the favorite victim. Dilute alcohol with equal parts of water; use a toothpick wrapped in cotton to touch each insect with the solution.

Some plant pests live in the soil, attack the roots of plants. Most common are spring-tails and fungus gnats. To control, dust the soil surface with DDT or chlordane. Isolate the plants until you're sure all of the pests are gone.

grooming of plants

Their good looks will be your reward.

When vining plants grow large, they look better grown on a support. English ivy has been trained to climb a trellis, just like one for a rose, only smaller. Make one the size you need and paint it to match the color of the foliage.

Encourage plant to put out new shoots by pinching off some of the end growth; reroot and plant cuttings in pot if growth at the base seems sparse.

On all flowering plants, remove the blooms as soon as they begin to wither. Don't let them go to seed and waste the plant's energies. Some, like coleus pictured, put up a flower shoot that also should be pinched off to improve the attractiveness of the plant.

Keep your plants clean and they will grow better, look better. A soft, damp cloth makes the best duster for the big-leaved plants like this fiddleleaf fig.

Support each leaf from the back with one hand as you give it a gentle dusting with the other.

If the leaves show water spots, sponge with a mild detergent solution. Rinse with lukewarm water.

Any plant not too big to be moved to the sink will benefit from an occasional complete shower bath as a supplement to the regular dusting of its foliage.

Use a bulb spray or the hose attachment on a kitchen sink to do this job. Always use lukewarm water; cold water spots leaves.

Hairy-leaved house plants, such as African-violets, Rex begonias, or gloxinias may either be washed with a lukewarm spray or brushed to remove dust.

A pipe cleaner or small soft-bristled paintbrush is a very satisfactory cleaning tool. Brush gently toward tips of leaves.

Chapter 6

How to multiply your plants

By seed

Stem cutting

Leaf cutting

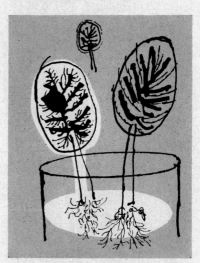

Asparagus fern
Avocado
Bromeliads
Cactus
Coleus
Crossandra
Gloxinia
Impatiens
Lemon
Kalanchoe

Chinese-evergreen
Christmas cactus
Coleus
Crown of thorns
Dieffenbachia
Dracaena
English ivy
Fiddleleaf fig
Grape-ivy
Impatiens
Nephthytis
Peperomia
Rubber plant

African-violet
Cissus*
Gloxinias
Kalanchoe*
Peperomia
Philodendron*
Rex begonias
Sansevieria
Scindapsus*
Sedum species
*Cutting must include leaf
  bud as well as leaf.

Everyone who develops more than a passing interest in house plants wants to try his hand at propagating new ones. The excitement of watching a cutting take root and grow into a mature plant never wears off.

The commonest and easiest way to increase the majority of true house plants is by a stem cutting. There are few which do not respond to this method.

Second most frequent is division. If a plant sends up a number of branches at the surface of the pot—such as the fern—it can probably be cut into several portions, and each part potted singly, as a new plant.

Growing house plants from seed—in contrast to plants for the garden—is least used method. Once seeds have germinated, it is difficult in ordinary home surroundings to supply the degree of humidity needed, keep temperatures low enough. But for anyone who can overcome these obstacles, it is an inexpensive way to grow plants in quantity.

Consult the plant check lists below to see how you can multiply your favorites. In a number of cases there will be several ways. Pictures and text in the remainder of this chapter show you how to handle each of the methods of plant propagation with success.

Division

African-violet
Asparagus fern
Aspidistra
Airplane plant
Begonias
Boston fern
Bromeliads
Chinese-evergreen
Echeveria
Maranta
Pandanus
Sansevieria
Strawberry saxifrage

Runners

Airplane plant
Apostle plant
Boston ferns
Bromeliads (some species)
Pickaback plant
Strawberry saxifrage

—Or by offsets:
Any plant which you can start by division.

Air layering

Dieffenbachia
Dracaena
Fiddleleaf fig
Rubber plant

—Or any plant which you can start by means of a stem cutting.

Soil mixture and equipment you'll use to grow new plants

Starting new plants indoors can be done on small or large scale, depending on the space you can devote to it and the number of new plants you want. A single clay pot accommodates a number of cuttings or seeds. For quantity, a flat is more satisfactory.

Basic care is the same

Whatever method of plant propagation you choose, the basic care is the same. Start with clean, strong parent plants. Don't try to root diseased, insect-infected cuttings. If you're beginning with seed, use the best quality you can purchase.

Use clean pots or seed flats and fresh rooting materials. Don't re-use sand or vermiculite which may be infected.

Keep the rooting mixture moist, never wet, and have humidity as high as possible. Use glass lids or plastic covers to trap moist air. Dust with ferbam if disease starts.

A light soil mixture is best

Pot each cutting separately as soon as it has formed good roots. Use a light soil mixture consisting of equal parts of sharp sand or gravel, peat, and garden soil. Add compost to the mixture if it's available. Don't feed new plants until growth starts.

A set of small hand tools is convenient if not essential to the indoor gardener. The pointed tool included in this group is a dibble, handy for making holes in the soil of right size to take a cutting.

A pencil, kitchen spoon and fork make good working substitutes for such a set.

Here are all the basic ingredients needed for rooting and potting new plants. The plastic sheet can be formed into a tent or cover to keep humid air about seedlings or stem cuttings while they form roots.

Plastic and sphagnum moss are also used for air layering (described later).

Use vermiculite (or perlite) or coarse sand for rooting cuttings.

Combine peat, soil, and sand or gravel in varying amounts to suit the particular needs of the new plants you are growing.

SPHAGNUM   PLASTIC SHEET   PEAT   SOIL   SAND   VERMICULITE

Wooden flats are practical for large-scale propagation

Good size for wooden flat is about 12 inches square and 3 inches deep. Rot-resistant materials, such as redwood or cedar, are best. Pine, if it is well seasoned, is satisfactory.

Keep flats from spreading by reinforcing with angle irons. Flats need cracks for drainage; or bore several ½ inch holes in the bottom.

Layer of brown paper will prevent soil from seeping out. Slits in paper will permit excess water to escape. Put in layer of coarse gravel or broken pots before filling with soil.

For a small number of seeds, use a clay pot with glass cover

Because insufficient humidity is the greatest hazard in successful germination of seed grown indoors, a glass lid or plastic cover is helpful.

Small seeds need no soil cover and may be sprinkled directly on surface of fine-screened sphagnum moss. They germinate best on a damp surface.

Wick watering or watering from the bottom is advisable so as not to disturb or wash out the fine seedlings.

As seeds germinate, gradually slide pane off and let air circulate.

Bottomless plant bands make it easy to shift young plants

Good for growing seedlings up to a size where they are ready to shift into small pots, plant bands let you move young plants with minimum disturbance of tender roots.

Fit the bands into the flat; fill with soil mixture and sow seeds. Pull out all but the strongest seedlings from each of the plant bands.

This same arrangement is also practical for starting a large number of tuberous begonias indoors.

You can manufacture your own plant bands from milk cartons.

The miracle of growth changes seeds into plants

Increasing plants by seeds is among the most dramatic and rewarding methods of propagation. Given light, warmth, moisture, and the passage of time, tiny seeds sprout, take root, grow into young plants, at the least possible cost.

Growing new plants from seeds

For success with starting seeds indoors, give them a porous and well-drained soil

SPHAGNUM

VERMICULITE

SOIL 2 PARTS

SAND 1 PART

PEAT 1 PART

←

You can use sphagnum moss, vermiculite, perlite, or a soil-sand-peat mixture for starting seeds. Moisture, proper aeration, good drainage, and a sterile planting mixture are vital to young plants.

→

Even fresh seeds need disease protection before planting. Dusts for this purpose are available at garden supply stores. Use amount shown on knife for one packet.

1 Soil for seeds should be fine and free of lumps, weed seeds. If using compost or garden loam, it is well to sift it through screen before combining with peat and sand.

Soon your seedlings will become crowded, need to be transplanted and spaced apart in another flat or pot

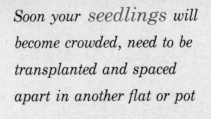

2 Provide for bottom drainage. Fill container with moistened growing medium. Jostle to settle. Tamp down with a brick to leave ⅜ inch room at top rim for watering.

5 While seeds are germinating, keep the flat covered with glass or plastic and paper to furnish darkness. Leave crack for circulation of air. Move to sun as sprouts appear.

3 A ruler or short piece of lath is handy for marking off rows in your flat. Space rows about 2½ inches apart. For the very small seeds, omit this step; scatter on surface.

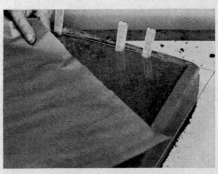

6 As plants grow, keep thinning out weaklings to promote development of sturdy ones. Pencil or dibble makes a good pry for lifting seedlings without damaging roots.

4 Drop seeds in rows ⅜ to ½ inch apart. If growing several varieties in one flat, use plant stakes to identify. Sift sphagnum moss or sand over planted rows of seed.

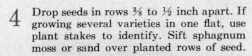

7 When first true leaves appear, transplant to another container. Make hole in potting soil with pencil or dibble so tender roots can be set in place easily. Water well.

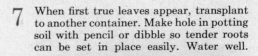

154

Propagation by
stem cuttings

Plastic bag traps humidity

Eliminate troubles with wilt by enclosing pot and stem cuttings in a plastic bag during the time when they are taking root.

Hold bag in place with a rubber band that can be removed and replaced easily if the cuttings require watering.

Ivy is but one of many house plants that may be reproduced by stem cuttings

1   Roots develop best just below the point where a leaf joins the stem. Make your cut there. Cuttings should be from 4 to 8 inches long. Remove bottom leaf or two so as to have about 1½ inches of bare stem for inserting in the rooting medium.

2   Fill clay pot with damp vermiculite, perlite, or sand. Treat ends of cuttings with a root-promoting powder, if desired. Insert stem ends in rooting medium. Water and keep in cool location, in bright light but not in direct sun, until rooted.

3   After about 3 weeks, remove one of the cuttings to check root development. Time needed is variable, but it shouldn't take more than 5 or 6 weeks to produce roots of this size—large enough to warrant transplanting to a separate pot.

4   Select a pot of proper size—not over 4 inches for single cutting. Supply bottom drainage. Spread roots and fill in with potting soil. Firm down; water. Even if plant normally requires sun, keep new plant out of sun for first few days.

Propagation by leaf cuttings

Root leaf cuttings in water, sand, vermiculite, or perlite

Cover a jar with foil or wax paper; pierce holes to accommodate leaf stem. In water, roots form in from 3 to 6 weeks, much more rapidly in sand, vermiculite, or perlite.

When roots are well established—like those pictured—transfer leaf cutting to standard potting soil. New growth will appear and the original leaf will eventually wither away.

Big-leafed begonia and some other plants can be rooted from leaf sections. Cut so each unit includes a part of the main vein. Cut off the tips to reduce wilting problem.

When rooting in sand, vermiculite, or perlite, about ⅓ of the cutting should be submerged. Check root formation as for stem cuttings; transplant when roots become established.

Another kind of leaf sectioning

Choose a prominently veined begonia leaf with a 1-inch stem; insert stem in sand. Anchor leaf in place, face up, with toothpicks.

Use a sharp knife to sever each of the main veins. Cover with plastic film until the new plants develop at points where veins have been cut; repot new plants in soil.

Propagation by
dividing roots

*House plants may be divided any time,
though spring, when new growth is
about to begin, is most auspicious*

Division is one of the least complicated ways to increase a collection of plants. It consists merely of separating an existing plant into two or more sections, and then potting each part individually.

Any plant that grows in clumps and has a separate root system for each of its parts below the soil can be divided into two or more portions. Whenever a plant belonging to this group is in need of repotting, decide whether to shift it or divide it.

The decision ought to be based on the looks of the plant itself—whether it has an "overgrown" appearance; and its comparative size in relation to its setting.

Look at your plants with an eye to their needs. Do they need dividing? The two plants at right in the picture above are just reaching an attractive size—they may be divided, but they won't benefit from it. But the three on the left will look better—and grow better—after dividing. Follow the three steps below to give older plants a new lease on life or to get a new crop of your favorite house plants.

1 To remove plant from pot, turn it upside down; give pot rim a quick, sharp tap on the edge of a table. Soil ball, held intact by the roots, will slide out with no difficulty.

2 Shake the soil from the roots so you can see where the stems join the main plant. Select sections with good roots of their own that you can separate from the old plant. Pull the sections apart gently, or cut apart with a knife, if this is necessary.

3 Plant new sections in the same way as for any of your house plants. Use porous potting soil, firming it about the roots. Water thoroughly. Keep out of sun for a few days.

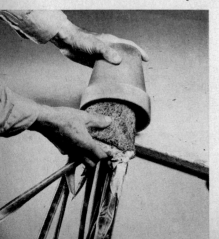

Propagation by
runners

*A cinch to propagate are plants
that send out aerial runners
forming new plants at their ends*

Some house plants, like this strawberry saxifrage, form new plants on runners. To get plant to root, just pin the runner to moist soil in a small pot placed nearby.

Roots will form quickly in a light mixture containing lots of peat and coarse sand. Keep the soil continuously moist and in a few weeks new roots will have become established so that you can cut the runner.

Propagation by
layering

*To compensate for loss of
bottom leaves on plants,
use the process of air-layering*

Cut lengthwise notch in stem of plant that is to be air-layered, at point where you'd like new roots to grow. Wrap in very moist sphagnum moss; hold in place with plastic.

In from four to six weeks, moss ball will be filled with new roots. (Check to see that moss remains moist; add water if necessary.) Cut off below roots and pot up. Save old plant. It will produce new top if you continue to water.

Convenient *glossary* of plant terms

Bloom. In addition to the common meaning of a flower, this word is also used to describe a whitish substance on the leaves and stems of a plant which rubs off on handling.

Bract. A leaflike part associated with flowers and sometimes inaccurately called a petal, as in the poinsettia and shrimp plant.

Bulblike. Plant which bears some resemblance to a bulb but is not a true bulb.

Cold-treated. The term describing a commercial process during which bulbs are stored at controlled temperatures, for fixed periods, to induce flowering at an earlier than normal time.

Compost. Organic matter made up of fermented or decomposed materials, such as leaves, grass.

Crown. Point at or just below the soil surface where stem and root join.

Cut back. To cut or pinch off growth at tips of plants, to encourage development of side growth.

Cutting. Any part of a plant that is used to propagate new ones—leaf, stem, or root.

Damping off. Disease of seedlings caused by several fungus parasites. Seedlings wilt and topple over, appear water soaked.

Dormant. The rest period of a plant or bulb, during which growth ceases or slows down.

Dry off. Process in which soil is permitted to become so dry that foliage is dropped and plant becomes dormant; used with many bulbs.

Established plant. Plant which is well enough rooted to take hold and thrive without intensive or extraordinary care.

Flats. Shallow boxes for growing seedlings.

Force. To make a plant bloom before its natural season of blooming has arrived.

Germination. The first growth of a seed.

Humus. The decomposed organic material which is capable of holding large amounts of plant nutrients and moisture. Usually added to garden soil and sand to make a potting mixture.

Leggy. Said of a plant which is tall and does not branch as it should, and which often has no leaves except at its top; the condition is usually caused by lack of pinching back at the proper stage of growth, or by too little light.

Lobe. Portion of a petal or leaf that divides the whole to about its middle.

Midrib. The main rib of a leaf which is a continuation of the leafstalk.

Node. Point on stem from which leaves arise.

Offset. A short side shoot which is used for purposes of propagation.

Palmate. Lobed, divided, or ribbed in a manner which resembles a hand; said of a leaf.

Pinch back. See "cut back" above.

Plunge. To lower a potted plant into water so that the pot is almost entirely submerged.

Pricking out. The first transplanting of seedlings from original seedbed into other flats or into individual pots.

Propagate. To increase plants by such methods as division, cuttings, or from seed.

Runners. Thin, wiry shoots that a plant sends out, which produce new plants at their ends.

Shift. To take a plant out of its pot and replant it in one of larger size.

Slip. A stem cutting taken for the purpose of propagating a new plant.

Standard potting soil. As used in this book, a potting mixture consisting of one-third each of soil, sand or gravel, and peat moss.

Sterilization. Treating soil in order to destroy organisms in it.

Tamp. Lightly firm down fresh soil with the hands or with a flat utensil.

Tendril. The slender prolongation of a leaf or stem which clings to a support.

Transplant. To remove a plant from the place where it is growing and move to new location.

Tuber. Swollen underground stem which bears eyes, such as potatoes.

Variegated. Including more than one color; having a dappled appearance.

Whorl. A group of three or more leaves or flowers appearing at one node, in a circle.

Syringe. To wash a plant by means of a fine spray, covering foliage.

Wick-watering. Watering of pots or flats from the bottom by means of cloth or fiberglass wicks inserted in soil and extending downward into a water reservoir beneath.

A

Index

B

C

D

E-F

G

Boldface numbers indicate pages containing major cultural information.

Boldface numbers indicate pages containing major cultural information.